SLAY YOUR GIANTS

NELL W. MOHNEY

Slay Your GIANTS

LIFE LESSONS FROM THE STORY OF DAVID AND GOLIATH

DIMENSIONS
FOR LIVING
NASHVILLE

SLAY YOUR GIANTS
LIFE LESSONS FROM THE STORY OF DAVID AND GOLIATH

Copyright © 2007 by Dimensions for Living

This book is printed on acid-free paper.

Library of Congress Cataloging-in-Publication Data

Mohney, Nell.
    Slay your giants : life lessons from the story of David and Goliath / Nell W. Mohney.
    p. cm.
    ISBN 978-0-687-49106-3 (binding: paperbck, adhesive perfect : alk. paper)
    1. David, King of Israel. 2. Goliath (Biblical giant) 3. Bible. O.T. Samuel, 1st, XVII--Criticism, interpretation, etc. I. Title.
    BS1325.52.M64 2007
    248.4--dc22

                                                                2007017137

07 08 09 10 11 12 13 14 15 16—10 9 8 7 6 5 4 3 2 1
MANUFACTURED IN THE UNITED STATES OF AMERICA

CONTENTS

INTRODUCTION

Julia no longer lived in our city, so I was thrilled when she called and invited me to lunch while en route to her parents' home in a northern city. *Would she still be as vivacious and friendly as I remembered her?* I wondered. I soon found out that she wasn't!

In answer to my greeting, "Julia, how are you?" she replied, "I'm fighting huge giants in my life." As I listened, she listed them: a rebellious teenage son, for whom alcohol was a growing problem; a formerly strong marriage that was being affected negatively by their son's behavior; and a resultant sense of defeat and lack of self-esteem on her part. There was no doubt about it: My friend Julia was fighting some real giants.

We talked for hours, and from time to time her eyes filled with tears as she described the son who had made a one-hundred-eighty-degree turn from the happy, gregarious, courteous little boy I remembered. The change seemed to start when, after a family move, he had had to change high schools. His need to be liked and accepted by his peers caused him, unfortunately, to choose a group in which alcohol was the accepted norm. Despite a stay in rehab, their son's drinking was out of control. Most of all, Julia was deeply worried about the tension their son's problems had caused in her marriage. Basically, she and her husband disagreed about how to relate to Jimmy in regard to his problems.

Together we worked out an action plan that would help her to relax and draw upon her spiritual resources, find ways she could more clearly understand her husband's position, and compromise or soften her position about her son.

She needed someone to hear and understand her feelings as a mother. She needed "psychological air" in order to think clearly.

She also needed a reminder to anchor herself in a bedrock faith and to "trust in the LORD with all [her] heart and lean not on [her] own understanding" (Proverbs 3:5 NIV).

I came away from that encounter convinced of three things. First, all of us face "giants" from time to time in our lives. No one is exempt. Ironically, these giants often confront us when we feel confident that we have our lives in great working order.

Second, we need to revisit and learn from the biblical story of David and the giant Goliath. Because David fought Goliath and won, so can we! David's greatest weapon was an unswerving trust in the God of Abraham, Isaac, and Jacob. He had lived his young life in close relationship with the Almighty and had witnessed God's protective power as he had kept lions and bears away from the sheep he tended (see 1 Samuel 17:34-37).

Third, the Christian faith provides the resources we need for battle. Though David lived before Christ came into the world, we are fortunate to live in an era when God's grace, power, and presence have been fully revealed through his Son, Jesus Christ. When we accept Christ's twin gifts of salvation and eternal life, we are empowered by the Holy Spirit and have the spiritual equipment to fight any giant and win.

This book deals with some of the common giants we face in life—such as grief, depression, procrastination, stress, perfectionism, resentment, jealousy, loneliness, inferiority, and disappointment—and offers practical, everyday actions that will help us to successfully fight them. Each chapter ends with a section called "Digging a Little Deeper," which provides reflection/discussion questions to help us clarify the problems we face and scriptures to remind us of our spiritual resources.

Whatever giant you may face in life, be encouraged by the good news that through Christ, we have the resources to be "more than conquerors" (Romans 8:37). By his words and actions, Jesus came to tell us that "our God . . . is able to deliver us" (Daniel 3:17).

Chapter 1

THE STORY OF DAVID
AND GOLIATH

*But David said to the Philistine, "You come to me with sword
and spear and javelin; but I come to you in the name of the
Lord of hosts, the God of the armies of Israel, whom you have
defied. This very day the Lord will deliver you into my hand."*
(1 Samuel 17:45-46)

My encounter with Julia caused me to go home and reread the
biblical story of David and Goliath in its entirety. It is not only an
inspirational story but also a fascinating character study offering
some valuable life lessons that can help us as we face giants in our
own lives.

A Boy Fights a Giant

Scene 1: David Takes a Care Package to His Brothers

Jesse, an Israelite, had eight sons. The three oldest were in Saul's
army; four tilled the soil with their father; and David, the
youngest, watched over and cared for the sheep. Like any contem-
porary father, Jesse was concerned about and prayed for the three
who were in harm's way in battle. Without access to television or
postal service, Jesse longed to know how they were doing. So from
time to time, he sent a "care package" to his sons in the army.

As the drama opens, Jesse has instructed David to go and check
on his brothers and bring back word. My guess is that he hoped to
receive a letter from each of the three. David also is to take a

bushel of roasted grain and ten loaves of bread to his brothers and cheese for the captain of the army (see Samuel 17:4-7). A smart father!

In scene one, we find young David engaged in a mundane task—taking food to his brothers in the army. Similarly, we are often engaged in normal, everyday activities when we encounter our own giants—such as grief, depression, stress, resentment, loneliness, or disappointment.

Scene 2: David Meets Goliath

After the long walk, David arrives at the valley of Elah where the Philistine army is camped. He hears everyone talking about the Philistine giant, Goliath, who is nine feet tall—and this is before the days of steroids, growth pills, and basketball teams! Goliath wears a bronze helmet, a two-hundred-pound coat of mail, and bronze leggings; and he carries a bronze javelin, which is several inches thick. His armor bearer, who carries a huge shield, walks ahead of Goliath (see 1 Samuel 17:4-7).

As David watches, Goliath appears and shouts his challenge for a Hebrew to come and fight him. If Goliath wins, the Hebrews will become slaves of the Philistines, and vice versa. Young David can't believe that no one in the army of the Lord has the courage to fight the giant. Saul has offered incentives—a large purse of money, one of his daughters' hand in marriage, and permanent exemption from paying taxes (see 1 Samuel 17:23). This is the ultimate concession for a politician at any time in history!

In scene two, we learn that we have to face our giants. We can live in denial by pretending that they are not there; but if we don't face them, we'll be intimidated and, ultimately, defeated.

Scene 3: David Fights Goliath

Despite the pleas of his brothers, David goes to King Saul and says in effect, "Don't worry about anything. I'll take care of the Philistine." Saul takes one look at the teenager and says, "Don't be ridiculous! You are nothing but a boy, and Goliath has been in the army since he was a boy." Then David tells Saul that God will protect him just as he has protected him while keeping sheep. He says, "The Lord who saved me from the claws and teeth of the lions and bore me safe, will bear me safe from the Philistines" (1 Samuel 17:32-37 TLB).

We know the rest of the drama—how David rejects Saul's armor and goes forth with five smooth stones, his sling, and a mighty faith in God. He calls out to the giant, "You come to me with a sword and a shield, but I come to you in the name of the LORD, the very God you defy. Today, the LORD will conquer you and Israel will learn that the LORD does not depend upon weapons to fulfill his plan. He works without regard to human means. He will give you to us" (1 Samuel 17:45-47, author's paraphrase). Psychologically, that's good stuff!

And that is exactly what happened. As 1 Samuel 1:50 tells us, "So David triumphed over the Philistines with a sling and a stone. Without a sword in his hand, he struck down the Philistine and killed him with Goliath's sword" (author's paraphrase).

David's Threefold Strategy

As I read the story, it occurred to me that all of us fight giants that intimidate us and cause us to be less than God created us to be. Yet there is hope. If we will become like David, we not only can face our giants but we can also slay them—overcome them—permanently! To become like David, we need to do three things:

1. Reject the Armor of Others

As we face the giants that attack us at different times in our lives, we can't simply observe how most people fight a similar giant and seek to use their armor. Just as David knew that Saul's heavy armor would not work for him, so also we must reject the world's armor of hatred, revenge, or lust as being not right for us. Instead, we can read widely about our giants and learn from other people of faith who have fought and won similar battles. These persons of faith—those of today as well as those of Bible days—

can give us practical suggestions about winning the battle in a manner pleasing to God. From their suggestions, we can choose what is right for us.

In addition to looking to the example of others, we should remember the armor that Paul suggests in Ephesians 6:13-18: truth, righteousness, peace, faith, salvation, God's Word (the Bible), prayer, and perseverance. We must choose our armor in light of the Christian gospel and allow God to tailor make it perfectly for our unique circumstances.

For example, once when I was fighting the giant of fear, I recalled relevant scripture verses such as "Perfect love casts out fear" (1 John 4:18); and "God has not given us a spirit of fear, but of power and of love and of a sound mind" (2 Timothy 1:7 NKJV). Still, it was not until I was ready to *believe* these truths and step out in faith that they became tailormade for me and for my circumstance. Though I had conditioned my mind with faith and scripture, which enabled me to believe that I could conquer the giant of fear, I didn't actually slay the giant until I did the thing I feared. In other words, I applied my belief through action. Let me share two instances of how this worked for me.

I used to be terrified of deep water, so I decided to take a swimming class. I got along fine in the shallow water; it was when the instructor told us to dive into deep water that everything in me rebelled. Yet, I knew that all my good intentions and biblical affirmations of faith would not be operative until I did my part and dove in. I closed my eyes and thought of the good life I had had until then, never expecting to come out of that water! Actually, I discovered that it is easier to swim in deep water.

Another fear was learning to speak publicly. I was even frightened of standing before a group and making a simple report. It was when I did my best and left the rest to God that I began to relax and even to enjoy the process. It took several years of making myself accept speaking invitations before I began to look forward to every opportunity, and eventually I came to feel that God was revealing that communication through speaking and teaching was one of my spiritual gifts.

So, rejecting the armor of others and finding what is right for us involves considering how we might learn from other persons of faith, examining the scriptures, and conditioning our minds with God's Word, and then taking action by faith.

2. Use Your Own Resources

In the biblical story, David was successful by using his own equipment—five smooth stones and a sling. We, too, have resources that can help us to fight the giants that threaten to defeat us. One of these resources is a healthy body. Though we may not be as physically fit as we'd like, we are alive and can strive to improve our physical condition or make the best of any limitations we may have.

When our bodies are ill, or even when we are fatigued, worried, or have no sense of well-being, we have no energy or motivation to face our Goliath. Because we are indeed one entity—body, mind, and spirit—what affects one of these aspects of our being will automatically affect the other two.

During the second week of hospitalization following surgery for ovarian cancer, I received my first chemotherapy treatment and began to dread nine more months of treatment. Then, into my hospital room came my friend Jane Isbell, who had had the same surgery and similar chemotherapy treatments. She was wearing a white running suit, and she looked healthy and radiant. In addition to sharpening my faith, she gave me one piece of advice: Work hard at keeping your body strong. She explained, "That will enable you to fight the disease." In the months that followed, I thought of Jane in that running suit whenever I didn't want to eat or exercise, and I did what she said.

Another resource we can use is our minds, which are far more complex than the most sophisticated computer. What is true for computers is true for the human mind: "garbage in, garbage out." We are bombarded daily with media messages of bad news, negative and evil events, concerns about terrorism, natural disasters, and economic distress. These messages affect not only our thoughts, but also our emotions, attitudes, and behaviors.

I know a very successful, positive Christian businessman who says that he never watches the news just before going to bed. Instead, he gets the news earlier in the day and, before going to sleep, he relaxes and reads the Bible—the one book he can read without having to stand guard over his thoughts. As he reads, he is encouraged by the promises of an omnipotent God. Consequently, his sleep is not disturbed and he awakens with optimism and a feeling of joy. He has learned the important lesson that we must stand guard over our thoughts, for it is through our minds and hearts that the Holy Spirit can move most effectively and guide us.

In addition to the Bible, there are some secular resources—sources of information—that can help equip us to defeat our giants, such as libraries, encyclopedias, and the Internet. These resources can provide us with valuable information about our giants and how to defeat them.

Most important, we have the resource of our will, which gives us the power to choose what we think. And as we've seen, what we think determines not only our attitudes but also our actions. It is when we use this resource that we are empowered to move from victim to victor.

3. Have a Mighty Faith in God

A mighty faith, as opposed to a weak faith, is rooted in confident belief in God and God's Word, unswerving trust in God, and faithful obedience to God. It is exemplified by steadfast and courageous day-by-day actions. I am inspired and encouraged when I read the stories of persons who have exhibited this kind of faith in God—persons such as Martin Luther, the founder of the Protestant Reformation; John Wesley, the founder of Methodism; Mother Teresa, who spent her life serving the poor and dying; Corrie ten Boom, who went to a concentration camp because of her commitment to Christ in helping Jewish families; and Nelson Mandela, who went to prison seeking to defeat apartheid, which prevented his countrymen from being recognized as equal and worthy citizens. All of these persons were able to fight social giants because of their mighty faith in God.

Because these and other well-known Christians have influenced us on our own faith journeys, we sometimes may feel that our own faith is small and inadequate. Remember Jesus' parable about the mustard seed. He said, "It is the smallest of all the seeds, but when it has grown it is the greatest of shrubs and becomes a tree, so that the birds of the air come and make nests in its branches" (Matthew 13:32).

So it is with our faith. As we continue to study God's Word, think, pray, and act, we find our faith growing stronger. Eventually ours becomes the kind of faith that encourages and blesses others on their journey—a mighty faith in God.

Now Let's Begin the Journey

In the following chapters, we will explore how we can use David's threefold strategy as we encounter personal and social giants that threaten our physical, emotional, mental, or spiritual well-being. Using the story of David and Goliath as our foundation, we will draw upon additional scripture passages in each chapter for further instruction in facing and fighting the various giants that threaten us. I hope you will find the book to be a practical guide to finding the "abundant life" Jesus describes in John 10:10. Enjoy the journey!

Digging a Little Deeper

1. Reread 1 Samuel 17. Why was David the only Israelite ready to fight the Philistine?
2. Put yourself in the place of young David as a devout follower of Jehovah when he encountered the giant Goliath. What would your emotions have been, and how would you have responded to them? As an adult, what is your first reaction when you encounter a "giant"? Is it fear, panic, resentment, or a quiet confidence that nothing can happen that you and God together

can't handle? How can we cultivate a growing confidence and assurance in God?

3. Ask yourself the following questions about David's threefold strategy:
   - *Reject the armor of others.* Have you ever tried to use someone else's pieces of "armor"—suggestions, advice, or strategies—and found that they were not right for you or your situation? Explain.
   - *Use your own resources.* What are some of your resources that, when used in cooperation with God's power, can make you "more than a conqueror"? How, specifically, could each of these resources benefit you?
   - *Have a mighty faith in God.* What steps can you take to strengthen your faith so that it becomes "a mighty faith"?

4. What is one "giant" you are currently facing? Why or how is this "giant" threatening to you? How might you follow David's threefold strategy to defeat this giant?

5. What strategies have you tried that haven't worked and should be left behind (worry, fear, panic, etc.)? How have these failed you?

6. What part of David's threefold strategy can you incorporate today?

Chapter 2

SLAYING THE GIANT
OF GRIEF

The king covered his face, and the king cried with a loud voice,
"O my son Absalom, O Absalom, my son, my son!"
(2 Samuel 19:4)

Have you ever hurt so badly that you literally felt numb? That feeling comes from loss—the loss of a loved one through death or divorce, or the loss of a job, a relationship, a home, or even a community after moving from a place where you have lived for years and in which you have deep roots. Loss is what I heard in a woman's voice one day when I answered the telephone and abruptly heard, "I didn't even get to say goodbye." Her call was in response to a note I had written expressing regret about the sudden death of her thirty-seven-year-old husband. As I listened, I realized that she was in what Wayne Oates calls the "opening the flood gates" stage of grief. It was Oates's book *A Christian and Anxiety* that had helped me understand the stages of grief as I had faced the death of our oldest son, Rick, years earlier.

Oates's book had reminded me that there are various stages of grief, such as trauma, shock, numbness, alternation between reality and fantasy, hesitancy to go places where we often went with the deceased, and allowing ourselves to be covered with God's love so that our tragedy can be transformed into triumph. Recognizing and understanding these stages is an important first step in fighting the giant of grief.

The Stages of Grief

The First Three Stages: Trauma, Shock, and Numbness

As Oates explains in his book, the first three stages of grief are trauma, shock, and then numbness. As I have learned from my own experience and from observing other grieving persons, these stages do not necessarily occur sequentially nor separately. For me, the first three stages occurred simultaneously since Rick was critically injured in an accident. Naturally, I experienced trauma and shock immediately. How could a healthy college student leave our home in the early afternoon for a meeting with our church's youth director and a few hours later be in a coma in the emergency room of a local hospital? It was surreal—like having a bad dream or being detached from the event and seeing it from a distance.

For two weeks, my husband, Ralph, and I were on an emotional rollercoaster. Some days Rick's vital signs gave us hope, but our hopes were dashed as day after long day the attending physicians found more internal injuries. On the day when Rick regained consciousness, we felt elated, though he couldn't speak because of a tracheotomy. Still, he could nod and squeeze our hands. Despite being warned by the doctors against too much optimism, we felt that our son was returning to us.

Shortly thereafter, another code 99 was called when Rick went into another cardiac arrest, and we were asked to step across the hall while the medical staff worked on him. One look at the doctor's face when he entered the small room in which we waited anxiously and prayerfully, and we knew the words that would follow: "The injuries were too great for Rick's life to be sustained in this world. Your son is dead."

In that moment, I couldn't wrap my mind around the sure knowledge that God has prepared a place for those who love him and are called according to his purpose. I believed that with every fiber of my being, but at the time, my physically and emotionally fatigued body went into numbness that lasted throughout Rick's funeral. I functioned, but almost robotically.

I'm convinced that God allows the numbness to protect us. If you had been with me at the time of our son's funeral, you would have felt that I was very much in control of my emotions. Actually, I was emotionally numb. Oh, there were some quiet tears—once when the minister read from three essays written recently by our son in an English class at the University of Tennessee at Chattanooga, and then when our younger son, Ralph, came home from the University of North Carolina for the funeral and eight of his classmates came along for support. But for the most part, I was numb and felt that I was taken over by the Holy Spirit, so that I could think clearly and help make plans for Rick's service. The numbness lasted throughout the visitation and service.

Others may experience these early stages of grief even more gradually, especially if their loved one has been terminally ill for months or even years. All of us may continue to experience shock or numbness in lesser degrees from time to time when the reality of the loss of our loved one becomes too painful.

In the weeks and months that followed our son's funeral, it was God's Word, prayer, and journaling that enabled me to resume my daily tasks and to believe that I would know joy again. I discovered that the best way for me to move through the early stages of grief was to continue my quiet time regularly whether I felt like it or not. My faith empowered me as I stopped often to give thanks for Rick's life and to recall biblical passages about life after death—passages such as "Jesus said to her, 'I am the resurrection and the life. Those who believe in me, even though they die, will live, and everyone who lives and believes in me will never die'" (John 11:25-26). Also, whenever I recalled seeing Rick's broken body, I thought of Paul's words about the body written in First Corinthians: "It is sown a physical body, it is raised a spiritual body" (15:44). It comforted me to know that Rick was very much alive and with God, and that his broken body was replaced by a whole, new spiritual body.

The Fourth and Fifth Stages: Fantasy and Denial

Oates says that the fourth stage of grief is alternation between reality and fantasy. It is easy to fantasize that the person who has died, or the one who has divorced you, will be coming in at any moment. For example, I found myself setting Rick's place at the table on several occasions. It is hard to allow our emotions to catch up with our minds.

A good friend who lost her husband three years ago told me that at five-thirty on most afternoons, she still listens for his footsteps on the porch. She also said that occasionally when she hears a good story, she thinks, *I must remember to tell that to Jim. He'll love that story!*

This is a tricky stage that, if we allow ourselves to linger, can lead to complete denial. Though all grieving persons experience denial to some degree, some people choose complete denial because reality is so painful. I know a woman who continued the practice of putting out her deceased husband's clothes for the day. She kept everything in the room exactly as it had been until the room became a shrine, and she developed a serious emotional illness.

Most of us have only occasional journeys into fantasy, and this is mainly out of habit. When I found myself setting Rick's place at the table, I would immediately take it up, give thanks for Rick's earthly life, and thank God for the new life Rick was now enjoying.

The fantasy stage goes away rather quickly as we replace fantasy with gratitude for having had the loved one in our lives and for the new life of wholeness he or she is now enjoying.

Denial takes longer to overcome. I'm convinced that denial is a protective measure that temporarily makes our pain bearable. As we attempt to move on with life (even when we don't feel like it), practice the presence of Christ daily, and observe the major holidays, the reality of our loved one's death becomes final.

The Sixth Stage: Opening the Flood Gates

Oates calls the sixth stage of grief "opening the flood gates," which is allowing our tears to flow and our feelings of anger and powerlessness to emerge. I'm convinced that if we push the feelings down, they will pop up in many ways at a later time.

For the past twelve years, I have spoken each summer at Lake Side, Ohio, the Chautauqua on Lake Erie. At one of my seminars, a middle-aged woman told me how, after her husband's death, she felt she must be strong for her three teenage children. After one week, she returned to her job, and at home she kept a stiff upper lip trying to make home life as normal as possible. Within six months, she began to feel signs of depression that worsened until, despite tranquilizers, she could no longer function. A lengthy period of rest was prescribed, plus medication, grief counseling, and faith restoration. We can't evade that lonesome valley—and the sooner we face the death or tragedy, the better.

When the friend I mentioned at the beginning of this chapter telephoned me, she had opened the flood gates of her feelings. It is important for our response to such a person to be one of quiet listening and affirmation. Under no circumstances should we disallow feelings by saying, "You shouldn't feel that way," or "You need to move on." Maybe they shouldn't feel that way, but they do, and those feelings must be dealt with before the person can move on.

We are very fortunate when we have one friend with whom we feel comfortable to open the flood gates of our feelings. Many churches have a shepherding program where a shepherd is assigned to the grieving person. In their visits, friendships are often formed, so that emotions can be shared. In my own case, it was Jesus, the ultimate friend, who became the confidant to whom I could pour out my feelings.

The Seventh Stage: Hesitancy

The seventh stage of grief according to Oates is the struggle we experience when we go places where we often went with the person we have lost. We hesitate to do this because we know that we will be overcome by grief. In my own journey through grief—and we must go *through* it, we cannot stop before we reach the end— it helped me to concentrate on happy memories and to talk about our son. I was surprised to find that some people never mentioned

Rick again to me. Perhaps it was because they thought it would make me feel worse. But he was still my son, and I wanted to talk about him.

In our family, we found that trying new things and making new traditions helped us through the difficult days—especially the holidays. For example, on Thanksgiving we chose to go out to eat for the first time ever. And at Christmastime, another member of our family hosted the Christmas dinner and gift exchanges. Some families go on trips. In our case, by the second year, we returned to regular traditions without too much difficulty. Other families choose to adopt their new alternatives as tradition.

Whatever you decide, try not to make special events or places occasions for renewed mourning. Of course, at times there will be unavoidable memories and feelings of sadness, but as Christians we find joy in knowing that we will see our loved ones again.

The Eighth Stage: Allowing God's Love to Cover Us

Oates suggests that the last stage in overcoming grief is to allow ourselves to be covered with God's love so that our tragedy may be transformed into triumph. The story of the oyster is somewhat analogous to this. When an irritant gets into the oyster's shell, the oyster surrounds it with fluids until it becomes a thing of beauty, a pearl. Similarly, only when we surrender our grief to God and walk freely with trust in God's purposes and steadfast love can God make something beautiful of our fragmented lives. Only then can we begin to understand the words of the apostle Paul when he wrote, "We know that all things work together for good for those who love God, who are called according to his purpose" (Romans 8:28).

If we are the friend of a grieving person, we can be the one who takes the casserole or extends an invitation to lunch. We can be the one who listens attentively when our friend opens the flood gates of emotion. We can make frequent, short, just-because-I-care visits, and we can encourage our friend to go with us to church or social activities. It is much easier for a grieving person to attend gatherings, even church, when someone offers to pick him or her up. In these ways, we actually become a conduit through which God's love can cover the grieving person.

Other things that helped me to allow God's love to cover me was to accept the kindnesses of friends—from enjoying their casseroles to allowing them to help us with thank-you notes. It also helped me to talk about Rick and the accident. Though I didn't always want to attend gatherings, I discovered that being with Christian friends enveloped me with God's love and ministered to my spirit.

My personal belief is that we can't force these stages. If we deeply desire to move through grief to wholeness, if we daily stay close to Christ, and if we take positive actions to help ourselves—such as joining a grief support group—then we can work through each stage as it appears. There will come a day when we feel normal again. We will never lose the loved one in our hearts, for we know that we will see them again. This enables us to move on with the plans God has for us on earth. Then we can become a blessing to others, turning our tragedies into triumphs. We can learn something about how to do this through the example of King David.

David Grieved for His Son

King David fought the giant of grief when his favorite son, Absalom, died. Handsome of face and with a full head of long hair, Absalom also had his father's genial personality and relational skills. What he didn't have was self-discipline, respect for his father, and a strong faith in God. As a result, the ambitious young prince planned a coup to have himself crowned king. Surrounding himself with his followers, he led a troop to the place where they believed King David to be. News of the coup reached Joab, who was David's top military commander. When Joab heard the news, he divided his soldiers into three groups and prepared for battle. As David saw each group off, he said to the captains, "Be gentle with the young man Absalom for my sake" (2 Samuel 18:5 NIV).

In a freak accident during the battle, Absalom's long hair caught in the braches of a tree, and he was left hanging there as his mount ran off without him. It was Joab who shot the fatal arrows through the prince's heart.

In 2 Samuel 19:4, we hear the tortured cry of a grieving father. Upon hearing of the death of his son Absalom he cried, "O my son Absalom, O Absalom, my son, my son!" David, the mighty king of Israel, had to open the flood gates of his feelings before he was able to continue his ordinary duties as king—even the simple task of thanking the soldiers who fought so courageously before him. His cries of devastating grief seem to indicate that he was in the fourth stage of grief—opening the flood gates. As I mentioned earlier, however, the stages of grief do not always occur sequentially.

Still, David may have experienced the first three stages— trauma, shock, and numbness—when he first heard that Absalom, the son into whom he had poured so much love, was trying to take over the kingdom and have him killed. This, I believe, is when his trauma and shock began. He must have felt sadness, even anger, at Absalom's betrayal. The biblical story suggests that David also experienced numbness because Joab had to remind him harshly that he must express his appreciation to the men who had fought so valiantly for him (2 Samuel 19:5-7).

Yet, as troops left to fight the defining battle, we sense David's love for Absalom as he asked each commander to be gentle with his son. Psalm 42 gives us a glimpse of David's mourning: "I say to God my Rock, 'Why have you forgotten me? Why must I go about mourning, oppressed by the enemy?'" (v. 9 NIV). Then David says to himself, "Put your hope in God, for I will yet praise him, my Savior and my God" (v. 11 NIV). Thus, David covered himself with God's love to enable himself to walk through the valley of grief and trust God for the future. We know that David was distressed in his spirit by his thoughts and memory (Psalm 55:1-2), yet he remained faithful to God. Even today David is still listed as Israel's greatest king. His Psalm 23 indicates that he eventually completed the grief journey.

We Should Never Waste Our Tragedies

In response to God's unfathomable love, we need to reach out to others even in our grief. Christians are not meant to waste their tragedies but to use them to help and serve others. What happens to us in life is not nearly as important as how we react to what happens. It is our choice.

We use our tragedies because Christ gave us the supreme example of taking the worst that could happen and allowing God to transform it into our redemption. On the cross, Jesus called out in a loud voice, "Father, into your hands I commit my spirit" (Luke 23:46 NIV). Then he breathed his last. It was then that the transformation was complete. When we do our best to fulfill the will of God and serve others for the sake of Christ, God can change our tragedy into triumphs.

I know a wonderful Christian man whose tragedy was that his wife decided to "find herself." In the process, she left her husband and their three small children. He reared those children into fine human beings, all of whom are strong Christians and productive citizens. Though he has not remarried, he regularly speaks to singles groups on life after divorce. He gives his audience hope and helps them to find a relationship with Christ, who turned his horrible crucifixion on Calvary into redemption for us all.

The story of Victor Frankl is a perfect example of this. Before the reign of Hitler in Nazi Germany, Frankl was a Jewish psychiatrist in Austria. He was a determinist, raised in the tradition of Freudian psychology, which states that what happens to you as a child determines and shapes your character and personality for a lifetime. According to this belief, the parameters of our lives are set and there isn't much we can do about it.

Then he and his entire family were imprisoned in death camps. His parents, brother, and wife died in the camps. Only he and his sister survived. In conditions too repugnant to report, Frankl discovered what he called "the last of the human freedoms"— the power to choose his response to terrible circumstances. The Nazis could control his environment and do what they wanted to his body, but he had the power to choose how it was going to affect him.

Using memory and imagination, he exercised his small embryonic freedom until it became larger and larger and he had more freedom than his Nazi captors. They had more liberty, but he had more freedom. For example, during the cold, hunger, and torture of his experience, he used his imagination to project himself into different circumstances of what he would do when he got out. He saw himself lecturing to students at the university and sharing the lessons that he had learned in the death camp. My guess is that those are the lessons he taught us all in his book *Man's Search for Meaning*.

Another example of the truth that our response to a circumstance is more important than what actually happens to us was evident in a small town where my husband, sons, and I lived. During one summer, two university students were killed in two different automobile accidents. These were only children, and both families were members of our church. After a period of mourning, the couples reacted entirely differently. One created a scholarship in their son's memory at the university he had attended, and the husband and wife became active in youth ministry, especially youth mission trips.

The other couple, a prominent professional family, couldn't seem to get through their grief. Eventually the husband had to leave his position at the bank because of his alcoholism. His wife was in and out of psychiatric hospitals. On closer observation, I believe that the first was a Christ-centered family who chose to turn tragedy into triumph.

This is not to say that it is easy. As I discovered in my own grief journey, we don't always finish one grief stage before moving to another in an orderly fashion. My emotions were close to the surface for many months following Rick's death. At times I felt I was doing unusually well when a tiny incident could open the flood gates of emotion. One day I was shopping in a downtown department store when a tow-headed little boy started running toward me. He looked so much like Rick at that age that I suddenly dissolved into tears.

Even so, I can offer you a word of hope. Be patient with yourself, and know that with the help of God, you *are* moving toward healing. Just as David slayed the giant Goliath through faith in God's power, so also we can slay the seemingly impossible giant of grief through faith in a God of the past, present, and future.

Digging a Little Deeper

1. Do you believe there is a purpose to grieving? If all of life were sunny and pleasant, do you believe we would ever discover our need of God or our own spiritual resources?
2. Read Isaiah 53:4. How does this verse, which describes the Messiah, relate to Jesus' promises in John 4:18? How are these promises fulfilled? How have you experienced the peace of the Holy Spirit in the midst of a storm?
3. If you are with someone who is in the "opening the flood gates" stage of grief, what is the best thing you can do and why?
4. The tendency of people who have been through sorrow or tragedy is to withdraw. How can we best encourage them to rejoin groups, get back to church, or just engage anew with life?
5. Read 2 Samuel 15:1-4 to understand the ways in which Absalom began to organize the coup against his father. Do you think that David's grief started when he learned of this treacherous act by his own son? Are there some things worse than death? Explain.
6. Tell of someone you know personally or know of who has been through great tragedy or deep hurt yet has allowed the love of Christ to cover them so completely that they continue to glorify God through a life of service. What have you learned from this person?

Chapter 3

SLAYING THE GIANT OF DEPRESSION

He lifted me out of the slimy pit, out of the mud and mire; he set my feet on a rock and gave me a firm place to stand.
(Psalm 40:2 NIV)

Have you ever had the Monday morning blahs seven days a week? Have you ever put one foot out of the bed and the other said, "I'm not coming"? Have you ever felt frustrated, fragmented, and overwhelmed? Have you ever felt that you needed your spiritual batteries recharged?

All of us have had these feelings at one time or another; but if the feelings become chronic, that's when we are in trouble. Then we are in a cycle of depression that will get deeper and deeper unless we do something to change our direction. So many people find themselves caught in this cycle, for depression is no respecter of race or nationality. It affects the rich and the poor. Young people suffer as much as adults. Suicide, incidentally, is the second leading cause of death among teenagers. Depression is indeed a pervasive problem.

Something I read in a devotional recently caused me to think seriously about the pervasive problem of depression. The scripture was Psalm 40, which provides graphic imagery describing depression. For example, Psalm 40:2 says, "He lifted me out of the slimy pit, out of the mud and mire" (NIV). Depression gives us the feeling of being bogged down—as if we're in quicksand.

I experienced the feeling of being caught in quicksand several years ago in Florida. Late one afternoon, my husband, Ralph, and

I drove by a deserted area of a beautiful, white, sandy beach. Since we had an hour before dinner, both of us said simultaneously, "Let's go sit on the beach and enjoy the sunshine." In order to reach the beach, however, we would have to walk through a section that looked like a marsh. No problem! We kept running shoes in the car, and it didn't matter if they got muddy. We'd simply slip back into good shoes on our way to dinner. Little did we know what awaited us. As soon as I stepped into the strange-looking sand, I knew why the beach was deserted. "It's quicksand!" I shrieked as I began to sink. When Ralph reached out to help me, he became engulfed too.

In retrospect, we are sure that passing motorists must have found our scene hilariously funny, but it was deadly serious and scary to us. Alternately we were clutching each other, sinking, screaming, and finally being pulled free by the sheer strength of Ralph's six-foot-two frame. Since then, I never read the second verse of Psalm 40 without thinking of our experience in that quicksand.

King David Experienced Depression

We can have the things that most people think will make them happy—health, financial security, a good job, support of family and friends, and faith—and still become depressed. In Psalm 40, we read that King David had the feeling of being in a slimy pit, which is a certain indicator of depression. We are not sure of the causes of David's depression, but with responsibilities as great as his, there surely would have been challenges—wars between Israel and neighboring countries, power plays by members of his staff, physical illness, family problems. It could be that the cumulative weight of these challenges caused David's normally optimistic attitude to change to discouragement and depression.

In the midst of David's problems, however, he never stopped giving thanks for God's goodness to him. This, I believe, enabled God to give David "a firm place to stand" (Psalm 40:2 NIV). Let's take a look at some of the easily recognizable signs of depression and how we can help those who are depressed, including ourselves.

Clear Signs of Depression

Though I haven't had severe depression myself, I have been mildly depressed on several occasions; and I know firsthand that depression can color our lives gray and rob us of joy and meaning. Also, I have worked with enough depressed people to know something of their feelings of helplessness as the world seems to give way beneath their feet. Severe depression makes an individual unable to function. It also may cause one to have sudden bursts of unexplained fears or a rather constant state of weepiness.

Another indicator of depression is a desire to sleep too much. Many psychiatrists see this as an unconscious desire to pull away from the world and its problems. Other depressed people seem to have difficulty in sleeping at all. Likewise, a sudden loss or increase in weight may indicate depression. And almost all persons suffering from depression lose interest in their usual activities.

Nathan S. Kline, pioneer in the biomedical treatment of depression, gives this perspective on depression in his book *From Sad to Glad* (Ballantine Books, 1987):

> Depression might be defined as the magnified and inappropriate expression of some otherwise quite common emotional responses. By way of analogy, you expect to find heart palpitations in one who has just run up a very steep hill, but something is decidedly amiss if such palpitations are found in one during a very sedate walk. So, too, with depression, all of us experience moments of sadness, gloom and pessimism as a natural result of certain circumstances. But in the depressed person, those feelings are all pervasive. They can be triggered by the least incident, or occur without evidence commensurate to an outside cause.

John, a man in his midthirties, was passed over for a promotion and went immediately into depression. His supervisor explained to all the employees in that department that, since the company was going toward globalization, they needed a person who spoke several languages. Because of a low self-image, John was sure that his supervisor didn't like him and believed that soon he would lose his job. That thinking was mere fantasy, but it could have become a self-fulfilling prophecy if John hadn't been wise enough to seek help for his depression and low self-esteem.

Angela is one whose depression had no apparent outside cause. Normally a happy young woman with a bright, sunny disposition, Angela looked sad and disengaged one Sunday in the class I was teaching. Thinking that she may have received some bad news or perhaps had broken up with her boyfriend, I put my arm around her shoulder and asked, "Are you all right?" Smiling wanly she replied, "I feel a little down today, but I'll be okay." The next Sunday, the symptoms appeared worse to me. When I telephoned her midweek, she was in tears; and I knew we were dealing with depression.

Fortunately for Angela, her problem was a chemical imbalance that could be taken care of by medication, good nutrition, and exercise. Over several weeks the sunny, happy Angela we loved began to reappear.

For some people, depression involves facing some unresolved issues from the past. In 1982, a well-known minister's wife spoke at a women's conference in our church. During the conference, she told of being hit suddenly by depression soon after she passed her fortieth birthday. After months of therapy, she began to recall an incident that had happened when she was only four. It had been so traumatic and deeply buried in her subconscious that it was only now beginning to surface. Her psychologist felt that since she and her husband had been unsuccessful in having children, her fortieth birthday signaled a loss of hope; and as she thought of children, her own childhood surfaced.

In a situation like this, it is extremely important to find help through a Christian psychotherapist or counselor. Later in the chapter we will discuss other times and signs when it is important to seek professional help. But first, let us consider some ways we can help others who are depressed.

How to Help a Depressed Person

One day I received a long-distance call from an out-of-state friend who was very depressed. One thing I've learned is not to give the depressed person quick assurance, pep talks, or the suggestion that she snap out of it. More than anything else, just being there to listen patiently and offer encouragement helps to relieve a person's sense of isolation and restore a sense of relatedness. Though I have learned these things through study, observation, and practice, perhaps I started learning them during my own hospital stay many years ago.

I had tried desperately without success to avoid major surgery, so I wasn't feeling very happy that I was in the hospital. In addition, my learning incident happened on the third day after surgery when I was feeling rotten. Into my room breezed a friend who was beautifully attired and looking like the picture of health. Suddenly my faded hospital gown seemed uglier than ever. To make matters worse, when she asked how I felt and I replied, "Not too well," she immediately told me how I ought to feel. She said that I should be grateful for all my blessings—grateful that the surgery was over, grateful that I lived in America, and on and on. It was only in retrospect that I realized why I felt so much worse when she left. She hadn't entered into my experience. She had disallowed my feelings and treated my surgery as if it were nothing more than a stumped toe. Listening and caring would have helped me so much more.

In addition to listening and caring, we can help someone whom we suspect is dealing with depression by inviting him or her to join us in activities that, if done alone, might be threatening to them. We can insist on their seeing a physician, especially if it is obvious that they are not getting adequate rest (too little or too much), or are not eating nutritionally, or are not exercising. Their depression might be caused by a physical condition. It also is very important that we encourage them to be involved in church. More than ever, a depressed person needs to feel the peace and power that comes from a daily relationship with Christ.

Coping as Christians with Depression

What can we do when *we* are the ones overtaken by feelings of gloominess and depression? In his book *Coping as Christians* (Upper Room, 1988), Maxie Dunnam suggests that we become totally honest about our feelings to God and to one other trusted friend. Pretending that these feelings are not there only allows them to pop up in other ways.

Second, he suggests that we stay close to significant others so that when we are engulfed by depression, they will take the initiative of relating to us even when we haven't the energy or the will to relate to them.

Third, he reminds us to use memory to affirm confidence and faith. A wise, older friend said to me once, "Hold on to your high moments of faith so that when you are discouraged, you can look back and see how God has led you through past difficulties." Perhaps five of the greatest words that occur throughout the Scriptures are "and it came to pass." No matter how dark the night seems, the morning always comes (see Psalm 30:5).

In addition to these three suggestions by Dunnam, I would like to add some others: exercising, relaxing, changing attitudes, reaching out to others, and giving praise to God.

First, any kind of physical exercise, even a short walk in fresh air, improves our circulation and helps clear our thinking. It also changes our perspective. When I am writing and get to a place where the creative juices are no longer flowing, I like to take a walk break. As I walk briskly and breathe deeply, I give not one thought to the writing I left behind. On the return walk, I slow the pace, taking time to listen, to see the wonders of God's creation, and to give thanks. Forty-five minutes later, I return to my writing feeling physically rested and renewed in spirit. The writing is no longer a chore but an opportunity. My perspective has changed.

Let me share a story that indicates a change of perspective through a change of attitude. In a sermon, the late Bishop Ernest Fitzgerald told of having an extremely hard day at the office. Personnel problems, a fire at one of their largest churches, and the death of a beloved colleague caused him to feel engulfed by despair. When he arrived home, his wife had bought "on approval" a beautiful new suit for him. After one look at the suit, the bishop commented, "That is not my kind of suit. I don't like the lines or the color. Please return it tomorrow."

The next day, things at the bishop's office went well, and he even had time for some golf in the afternoon. When he returned home, he saw that his wife had purchased another suit. Trying it on, he exclaimed, "This is perfect! I like the lines and the color, and it's a great fit. It is my kind of suit!"

Smiling, Mrs. Fitzgerald said, "Ernest, it's the same suit that was hanging there yesterday." The difference, said the bishop, was his perspective.

Another way to overcome depression is to reach out to others with a note, a telephone call, or a kind deed. These things help us feel related. They change our focus from our own problems to opportunities we have to touch the lives of others.

The Sunday school class of single adults that I teach has regular ways of reaching out to others. One way is our Inter-faith Hospitality. Once every three months we host homeless families for one week. We provide dinner and overnight accommodations for three or four families at a time. Each morning they are picked up and taken to Inter-faith headquarters so that the children may go to school and the parents may look for work or go to their jobs.

One businessman named David told me that he had signed up to help one evening but was feeling really down when he arrived. He was unhappy with his job and a bit resentful of those without homes because, as he said, "Everyone can get a job if they want one." That evening he was assigned to relate to the Bradford family. Only a year earlier, Mr. Bradford had owned a small house and had had a fairly good job; and his wife had been able to stay home and be there when the children came home from school. Then the accident happened that left Mr. Bradford in a local hospital for months.

The enormous hospital bills meant that Mr. Bradford lost his home and his car. His disability prevented him from returning to his old job. Both he and his wife were now working part time for minimum wage and were trying to save for at least a rental home. They were distressed to put their children through the experience, but Inter-faith Hospitality had given them hope that they could re-establish their home. They had a strong faith, no bitterness, and a great sense of gratitude.

David said, "I left that evening a changed man. I felt such gratitude for my job and my house. Also, I had a new respect for the people for whom life is a daily struggle. I had a new perspective."

Another way we can overcome depression is through praise. We can literally feel our spirits rising when we praise God—especially through singing. I'm sure you have your own favorite hymns or praise and worship songs, but some that have helped me when I am down include "Oh God, Our Help In Ages Past," "A Mighty Fortress Is Our God," "Great Is Thy Faithfulness," and "He Lives!" These songs have centered me in faith and reminded me of who I am. "Great Is Thy Faithfulness" was a congregational hymn sung at our church on the Sunday I returned after a battle with cancer. I sang it with tears streaming down my cheeks. Even today, fifteen years later, I get teary-eyed when I sing it. The faithfulness of our God is irrefutable.

When Ralph was serving his second church, he went through a period of depression. The church was growing rapidly—10 percent each year—and the number of staff members had not kept up with the membership growth. Ralph, who had never had any serious illness, continued to burn the candle at both ends. The result was both physical and emotional exhaustion, which, according to the doctor, was the cause of his depression.

A member of our congregation had a family home on Treasure Island near Tampa, Florida, and insisted that we go there for a few weeks. The freedom from heavy responsibilities and the beauty of the white beach and blue water of the Gulf combined to give us a total sense of relaxation. In addition, we took long walks; slept well; ate nutritionally; read inspirational materials, including the Bible; and sang hymns. In fact, Ralph says that the last words of one of the choruses we sang kept his mind focused on the wholeness that Christ was bringing into his life:

Thank you, Lord, for saving my soul.
Thank you, Lord, for making me whole.
("Thank You, Lord" by Seth and Bessie Sykes)

His restoration was so complete that he could continue the larger ministry to which he was called.

Zig Ziglar also tells of how music helped him in a time of crisis. Recently I listened to some audiotapes from a seminar led by Ziglar in which he told of the night his daughter died ("A View From The Top," Nightingale Conant Corporation, 2002). His daughter was in the hospital, and he would not leave her side. He did not sleep for twenty-five hours. After she died, he and his wife returned home. He tried to sleep but couldn't. He tried to read the Bible but couldn't. Finally, he went downstairs to the family room, stretched out on the floor, and put on a tape of the Gaither Trio singing comforting hymns. He said that he went to sleep immediately and, for the first time in months, slept soundly. Music truly can restore our souls.

Biblical Affirmations to Help When We Are Depressed

Throughout his earthly ministry, Jesus quoted scripture passages as he dealt with problems. One such time was when he was tempted by the devil in the wilderness (see Luke 4:1-13). Every offer that the devil made, Jesus countered with scripture, saying, "It is written . . ." and then quoting the scripture. This, I believe, gave Jesus the strength and clarity of mind to deal with the temptations.

In my own experience, I have memorized a number of biblical passages that I can call to mind immediately as I need them. When we are fearful, lonely, resentful, discouraged, or depressed, we can be empowered through God's Word. Truly, "Thy word is a lamp unto my feet, and a light unto my path" (Psalm 119:105 KJV). Here are a few passages that can empower us:

"Be still, and know that I am God" (Psalm 46:10 NIV).
"Thou wilt keep him in perfect peace, whose mind is stayed on thee" (Isaiah 26:3 KJV).

"Come to me, all you who are weary and burdened, and I will give you rest" (Matthew 11:28 NIV).

"Peace I leave with you; my peace I give to you. I do not give to you as the world gives. Do not let your hearts be troubled, and do not let them be afraid" (John 14:27).

"With God all things are possible" (Matthew 19:26 NIV).

"Trust in the LORD with all thine heart; and lean not unto thine own understanding. In all thy ways acknowledge him; and he shall direct thy paths" (Proverbs 3:5-6 KJV).

I have found that as I offer praise and affirmation, something within me begins to sing again. So, if your giant is depression, begin to do something to change it. We can become honest about our feelings to God and one trusted friend; we can stay close to significant others for support; we can use memory to affirm our confidence and faith; and we can exercise, learn to relax, and improve our attitudes.

If you are severely depressed, you also should see a medical doctor. You may need to take some medication temporarily, as well as see a professionally trained counselor.

If someone around you is depressed, begin to care and listen and help them feel less isolated. You also can invite them to join you in activities, to see their physician for a checkup, and to continue their involvement in church.

Whether the giant of depression is threatening you or someone you love, remember that our greatest help comes from the One who is able to do immeasurably "more than all we can ask or imagine" (Ephesians 3:20)!

Digging a Little Deeper

1. Have you ever experienced serious depression? If so, what was it like? What were some of the emotions you experienced (sadness, hopelessness, weepiness, etc.)?
2. Read Psalm 40:1-8. David obviously went through a period of depression. Though this psalm does not say what caused David's

depression, what problems do you think the king might have faced at this period in Israel's history?

3. How did David open himself to God's assistance, allowing God to lift him out of the pit? See verses 1-8.
4. What can you do to help yourself when you are feeling depressed?
5. How can you help a friend who is depressed?
6. What are some things you can do to prevent depression? After you have listed or discussed these ideas, choose a biblical affirmation—one listed in the chapter or one you select yourself—that you will say daily.

Chapter 4

SLAYING THE GIANT
OF PROCRASTINATION

As Paul discoursed on righteousness, self-control and the judg-
ment to come, Felix was afraid and said, "That's enough for
now! You may leave. When I find it convenient, I will send for
you." **(Acts 24:25 NIV)**

Professional thieves are often clever and cunning, and some are
even charming. One, whom I'll call Richard Bailey, had all three
attributes. He drove into the small town in which I grew up and
took it by storm!

Like Harold Hill in the movie "Music Man," he quickly became
a part of our community life, joining the church, a service club,
and the Chamber of Commerce. Children and youth thought he
was great fun, and seniors thought he was wonderful.

He was selling encyclopedias, and that by itself should have
been a tip-off. Usually it is college students who sell encyclopedias,
and Richard was thirty-two. We should have known better. When
he asked if we wanted to buy a set of encyclopedias, we should
have used the punch line: "No, thank you. We have a teenager who
knows everything."

But people in my town didn't know that punch line, and Richard
Bailey absconded with thousands of dollars from our citizens—
and not just from the sale of encyclopedias. When the city officials
tried to catch him, they discovered that he had more aliases than
a dog has fleas. He was a big-time thief!

Procrastination Is a Subtle Thief

There is a thief with whom all of us deal almost daily. He is just as believable as Richard Bailey—and even more subtle. His name is procrastination. He doesn't steal money or jewels or television sets or DVD players; he steals our time, our motivation, our very lives. In their place, he leaves excuses, alibis, rationalizations, and guilt. We often don't see through his ruses until it is too late. Many people go to their graves still procrastinating. Like most thieves, this one hits you when you are weak or when you relax your defenses.

Let's say, for example, that you have promised your children that you will help them build a playhouse on Saturday morning. You awaken with every intention of doing so, but procrastination reminds you that you have had a terrible week—that you are exhausted and need to relax. The thief doesn't suggest that you refuse to build the playhouse—only that you delay it until you are rested. The results: your children's trust in you is eroded (especially since this has happened before), you waste time during much of the day, and you end the day feeling guilty.

Interestingly, though we may temporarily feel guilty about this event, we often don't see that we have allowed procrastination to steal some of our most valuable possessions—our time, motivation, or a relationship of trust with a child. Neither do we realize that we are developing a habit pattern that will sabotage our best intentions.

Or let's say that your bathroom scales tell an unhappy story. You know that for your health's sake, you must reduce your caloric intake and cut back on fat and sugar. Today is the day to begin, but the thief's magic word is "mañana." He says, "Tomorrow is the day to begin. Today will be very stressful." So, you reach for another pastry and the grim thief has won another battle. You have succumbed to Scarlett O'Hara's philosophy: "I will think about that tomorrow."

Recently, I received an e-mail that told of a man announcing to his office staff that he was going on a diet. The following day he came into the office carrying a large coffeecake that was oozing with calories. "We thought you were going on a diet today," said the staff members.

"I was," said the manager, "but as I drove by the bakery, I saw this delicious-looking pastry in the window; so I prayed. I said, 'Lord, if you want me to have that coffeecake this morning, let me find a parking space right in front of the bakery.' Sure enough, there it was—on the eighth time around the block." We laugh about the manager's rationalization, but don't we also rationalize about things we need to do or not do so that the time of opportunity passes? Procrastination wins the battle.

Procrastination is so subtle that we often don't realize we are forging a habit that becomes harder and harder to break. It robs us not only of time and motivation, but also of the God-given ability of being decisive.

Procrastination Robs Us of Decisiveness

Procrastination robs us of our ability to be decisive. The psalmist tells us that God made us a little lower than the angels and crowned us with honor and glory (Psalm 8:5). With this comes the marvelous gift of being able to choose between good and bad, between right and wrong. In life's eternal decisions, we need to weigh all options, pray earnestly for guidance, and then decide. We can't sit on the fence about important life issues and ever make a difference for Christ.

In one of the "Peanuts" cartoons, Lucy asked Charlie Brown, "What are you going to be when you grow up?" Charlie Brown replied, "I'm going to be an evangelist." Whereupon Lucy asked, "What kind of evangelist?" Still trying to kick the football, which he can never get off the ground, Charlie Brown answered, "A wishy-washy one." We know that no evangelist and no Christian witness can be effective if they are indecisive or wishy-washy.

Deciding whether or not to postpone building a playhouse or to have another pastry are not eternal decisions, though they are significant choices for your family life and health, respectively. Determining your life's purpose, choosing a life partner in marriage, making a faith commitment to Jesus Christ—these are eternal decisions.

The biggest life decision we will ever make is whether or not we will come to faith in Jesus Christ. That decision determines our salvation, our values system while we are on planet earth, and our life after death. About this we can't be wishy-washy. We are either in or out. Some of the saddest words in the New Testament are found in the Book of Acts: "Then Agrippa said unto Paul, Almost thou persuadest me to be a Christian" (26:28 KJV). He couldn't be decisive in this eternal matter.

The wise and aging apostle John made God's feelings about indecisiveness crystal clear in a letter to the church at Laodicea: "I know your deeds, that you are neither cold nor hot. I wish you were either one or the other! So, because you are lukewarm—neither hot nor cold—I am about to spit you out of my mouth" (Revelation 3:15-16 NIV).

Felix Procrastinated about an Eternal Decision

In Acts 24, we read that Felix the Roman governor of Judea procrastinated about an eternal decision—a faith decision—until he came to a point of no return. A former slave, Felix had bought his freedom and had worked his way to a top position in the Roman Empire. A politician to the core, he had arranged for himself very advantageous marriages. Already he had been married to two princesses, but his eye was on the daughter of King Herod Agrippa I. Actually, she was married to Azizus, King of Emesa. Felix, with the help of a magician, had seduced her away from Azizus. She was the wife of Felix when Paul appeared before him.

From his missionary churches, Paul had taken an offering for the poor of Jerusalem, and he was meticulously following Jewish law when he was arrested. His defense before the Sanhedrin was vigorous and forceful, but there is no hint of self-pity or bitterness, which would have been natural for one who had been deliberately misrepresented.

When Paul was turned over to the governor, Felix obviously didn't believe the charges, but he wanted to pacify the Jews for political reasons. So Paul was imprisoned. Felix and his wife asked Paul to tell them about Christianity, and his presentation was so eloquent that Felix almost believed. Instead, he procrastinated and said, "That's enough for now! You may leave. When I find it convenient, I will send for you" (Acts 24:25 NIV).

Unfortunately, Felix never made the one decision that would have been most significant for him. Later he was removed from his prestigious position, and if it had not been for the efforts of his brother, Felix would have been executed. Since he didn't decide to come to faith in Christ, he had no power to strengthen and sustain him in his darkest hours—not to mention his eternal separation from God.

Don't "Sit on the Fence"!

Paul's experiences with Felix and King Agrippa emphasize the fact that we cannot sit on the fence, especially about eternal matters. Obviously, *any* weighty decision should not be made without thoughtful consideration and prayer. Yet some people spend their lives sitting on the fence, paralyzed into inaction. As a result, they end up on the sidelines of life, wasting their energies and talent. When they put off a decision about a problem that needs to be solved, the problem grows even larger.

In a company for which I presented a series of seminars, the CEO had a bud vase on his handsome desk. Instead of holding a rose, as one might expect, the bud vase held a thorn-filled branch. When I asked why, he told me that it was a reminder that problems need to be faced promptly and decisively. "If you touch the thorns tentatively, they will prick you," he said. "If, however, you grasp them quickly and all at once, they don't hurt at all." I didn't try it, so I don't know whether that is true or not; but I am certain that when we delay facing problems, they become more difficult to handle.

I have a friend whose son's behavior in middle school should have raised red flags in the mind of his mother. His grades were slipping downward, and the friends he chose didn't share any of the family's values. She discovered that he was not being completely truthful about even little things, and he refused to go to the church's youth group. My friend was a single mom with a stressful job and two other children.

Some of us who were her closest friends, and who had tried to help her in practical ways following the untimely death of her forty-year-old husband, tactfully tried to point out that there were red flags flying all around her son. In addition, a school counselor suggested counseling for the boy, as did the youth pastor at their church.

Though I don't understand my friend's thinking, I suspect she felt so overwhelmed with life that she didn't have the inner strength to deal decisively with her son, so she chose to deny the problem until a judge had to give a very harsh sentence to a drug-addicted high school student who had lost his way. It is definitely true that procrastination robs us of decisiveness.

Procrastination Robs Our Relationships

Sadly, procrastination affects all of our close relationships. I have the theory that no member in our family should leave the house without hearing "I love you." Granted, there are issues that need to be faced with our spouses and with our children, but not when there is no time to talk through the problem, and certainly not just before one is leaving the house. Also, I believe that no member of the family should receive more appreciation outside the home than at home. When another member has done well in an endeavor or reached a milestone, we should be the first to say, "Great job. I'm so proud of you." Procrastination should never cause us to forget the words of Paul to the Ephesians: "Be kind and compassionate to one another, forgiving each other, just as in Christ God forgave you" (Ephesians 4:32 NIV).

In my own life, I have found that I receive "God nudges" to help someone, or to take some constructive action, or to express appreciation. When I disregard these nudges, I always regret it. I'm still sad that I didn't take the time to tell my paternal grandmother how much she had influenced my life. She knew that I loved her, but I never expressed in words what she meant to me. Though I knew she wasn't feeling well, I had no idea that she was near death. So, I allowed the thief of procrastination to rob me of an opportunity I would never have again.

Many years ago when our children were preschoolers, I read an article that indelibly imprinted itself in my mind. The story was of an exuberant, hyperactive four-year-old named Sally, who was into everything. Often the mother had to say to Sally at bedtime prayers, "Don't you think you should ask God to forgive you for. . . .", and then a list of things would follow.

One day Sally tried to be good all day long—a gigantic undertaking for that four-year-old. That night her mother didn't have to say a word about asking God to forgive Sally, but the mother procrastinated about expressing appreciation. As she started downstairs, she heard a plaintive little voice ask, "Haven't I been a pretty good girl today?"

I was married and in my own home when my mother told me about an incident that had happened when I was eleven or twelve years old. At that time, many houses had crisp, white organdy curtains hanging at the windows. It was before the day of permanent press fabrics, so washing curtains wasn't a simple matter. You had to wash the curtains by hand, starch them, iron them, and place them carefully on a bed to keep them from wrinkling before they were hung. They were beautiful, but before legislation was passed for a cleaner environment, the white curtains didn't stay clean very long.

The incident to which my mother referred was a dinner conversation between my dad and us three children. Someone casually mentioned that the curtains were dirty. That statement didn't bother mother, because she had agreed. The thing that hurt her was that after all of her hard work to clean the curtains, no one had mentioned the clean curtains or expressed their appreciation. Her Christian faith enabled her to forgive us, but years later as we talked about various hurts we had experienced, that memory was still fresh.

To be sure, procrastinating about giving positive affirmation can hurt another person and thus negatively affect our relationship.

What to Do if Procrastination Is Your Giant

Have you ever wondered why in the biblical story of David and Goliath that David's brothers and the other soldiers in the army of Israel procrastinated about going to fight Goliath? Surely it must have been fear or lack of trust in God's power. David's mighty faith gave him the motivation to act courageously. Here are some practical steps we can take if procrastination is our giant.

Jeff Davidson of the Breathing Space Institute suggests several ways we can fight the giant of procrastination. Here is an adaptation of his suggestions:

1. Even though procrastinators may have some traits in common, such as the fear of failure or perfectionism, the tendency to put things off is mainly a habit; and habits can be changed. Determine to change your habit of procrastinating, and remember that it takes at least thirty days to break or make a habit.

2. Set specific goals. People who focus only on priorities (big picture intentions) don't get a lot done because they have no specific action plans. For these, you need goals. For example, if your priority is to be healthy, one of your goals could be "go to the Y on Wednesdays for a workout." Identify the areas in which you tend to procrastinate, and then set one or two specific goals that will help you to achieve your desires in each of these areas.

3. Avoid information overload. Don't try to collect every available piece of information before making a decision. Since there is always more to know, trust your instincts. This doesn't mean acting on a whim. It means collecting enough information to make an informed decision while using the knowledge and information that you have accumulated over the years.

4. Don't wait to be in the mood. Can you imagine a pilot saying, "I'm not in the mood to land this plane," or a mother saying, "I'm not in the mood to pick up my children from school"? Most

successful people produce on schedule no matter how they feel. The late William James, a professor at Harvard University, suggested an "Act As If" philosophy. He said that most people act on their feelings. For example, when a person awakens "onery," he or she will act "onery" all day. James suggested that if people decide how they are going to act—based on the Christian faith—and acts that way, their feelings will follow. As Shakespeare said, "Assume a virtue until you have it." In other words, if you don't feel very confident, act confidently until it becomes a part of your very nature. As Christians, our faith is based not on feelings, but on the fact that God loves us. John Wesley taught his preachers to "preach faith until you have it and then preach it because you have it."

5. Divide the project into smaller jobs. Jill Briscoe, Christian author and speaker, suggests that if you have to clean the garage, clean one corner at a time. You will procrastinate if you have limited time and try to clean the entire garage. It will seem impossible. If, however, you can clean just one corner today and another corner two days later, it will seem doable. Alan Lakein, who has written widely on time management, suggests that if you start with an easy job, then things will begin to fall into place.

6. Plot a course. As I write this, our granddaughter is planning to be married in five months. She and her parents have planned backward in order to move into the future with all bases covered. For example, they have listed what date to choose the wedding dress, get an announcement picture to the paper, order invitations, make lists of wedding guests, and so forth. It would seem overwhelming if they hadn't carefully plotted a course. (Adapted from Jeff Davidson, "How to Beat Procrastination," *Bottom Line Magazine*, March 2003)

In my own life, I have fought the giant of procrastination by doing three things consistently:

1. Every New Year's Eve, I have listed ten "great expectations" for the coming year in four areas of my life: physical, mental, spiritual,

and relational. I always give these expectations two tests. (1) Is there anything listed that will hurt me or anyone else? (2) Is there anything that is not in keeping with the will of God? If the expectations pass both tests, I go over them regularly in order to plant them in my subconscious and to stay focused. For each, I work on an action plan. Though I certainly haven't accomplished all of my great expectations, I have come far enough to pray the prayer: "Lord, I'm not what I ought to be; I'm not what I would like to be; I'm not what I'm going to be; but, thank God, I'm not what I used to be."

2. Each evening before retiring, I write down six things I plan to accomplish the next day, excluding regular chores such as washing dishes, making beds, cooking, and so forth. Without this plan, I am disorganized and waste time and effort. For example, my six things to do one day might include going to the grocery store, the cleaners, and the drugstore. Then I plan my route to include all three instead of doing them haphazardly.

3. In my morning quiet time, I read scripture and other inspirational material, and then I get quiet enough to listen for God's guidance and creative ideas. It's the way I "set my sails" for the day. My quiet time gives me the opportunity to go over the things I listed the night before and the motivation to get to work on them.

Procrastination is one of the most difficult giants to slay because we can rationalize that we are just postponing taking action, rather than deciding not to take action. Yet, sadly, the grand thief procrastination will have robbed us of time, motivation, decisiveness, and strong personal relationships. Let's recognize the giant for what he is and take practical steps to prevent his "breaking and entering" and destroying our lives. Most of all, let's use our spiritual resources to fight the battle.

Digging a Little Deeper

1. In what ways is procrastination a "thief"? List those things that procrastination has stolen from you—time, the use of talent, the

ability to be decisive, and so forth. What have been the ramifications or results of losing each of these things?

2. What do you think might be causing or contributing to your habit of procrastination? Could it be fear of failure or a tendency toward perfectionism? Could unreasoned anger be causing you to drag your feet? Is the problem resistance to a schedule? Is it simply that you are not organized? How might you seek to determine the cause? Through prayer and study, seek the reason you procrastinate; then take a few practical steps this week to defeat the giant and jump-start your fast forward gear.

3. Read Acts 20:24-27. What is the vivid example of a missed opportunity for Felix because of procrastination?

4. The practice of writing down our expectations for the coming year gives us the big picture of what we wish to accomplish for Christ. How is this helpful in determining our weekly and daily goals?

5. What might be some of the benefits of making a list each night of the most important things (other than regular responsibilities or chores) to be accomplished the next day? Do you see any possible drawbacks or negative outcomes of adopting this practice? If so, what are they, and why do you feel this way?

6. Why is it important to take time daily for Bible reading, prayer, and silence as we set our expectations and goals?

Chapter 5

SLAYING THE GIANT
OF STRESS

Do not be anxious about anything, but in everything, by prayer
and petition, with thanksgiving, present your requests to God.
And the peace of God, which transcends all understanding, will
guard your hearts and your minds in Christ Jesus.
(Philippians 4:6-7 NIV)

In the middle of a stress-filled day, have you ever echoed the
words of the title and theme song for the Broadway musical
"Stop the World! I Want to Get Off"? Research studies have
shown that many illnesses and diseases have stress-related ori-
gins, including colitis, ulcers, headaches, respiratory problems,
high blood pressure, depression, and some forms of cancer. In
fact, unmanaged stress is believed to be the leading factor in
homicides, suicides, child abuse, spouse abuse, and other aggra-
vated assaults.

In mechanics, stress is the measurement used to determine the
internal strength of a metal to withstand an imposed weight load.
Yield point is when the weight makes the metal stronger. Failure
point is when the strain exceeds the load-bearing capacity of the
metal. We are much like the stress measurement in mechanics. All
of us need a certain amount of stress to test our personal metal
and make us stronger. If, however, we are dealing with more than
we can adequately handle, we are not living the abundant life
Jesus promised in John 10:10.

Let's look at two different kinds of stress.

Different Kinds of Stress

First, there is good stress, *eustress*, which motivates us, inspires us, and brings out the best in us. Without eustress, we would be like soft, squishy marshmallows. I love the story of the mother who called her son three times to get up for Sunday school and church. No response. Finally, she yanked the covers back and said, "Get out of the bed *now*." A sleepy voice replied, "Give me three good reasons." In exasperation, the mother replied, "First, it's Sunday; second, you are forty-two years old; third, you are the minister." Though that is a humorous exaggeration, the fact is that most of us work better under some pressure.

Good stress can cause us to be more productive, but too much good stress occurring simultaneously can affect our health and well-being. We can lose sleep, become fatigued and irritable, and lose our zest for living. These symptoms, when accompanied by one or more major stressors, can lead to serious emotional or physical problems.

Second, there is bad stress, or *distress*. Distress occurs when our circuits are overloaded and we feel fragmented. Usually we recognize the symptoms of this kind of stress. Sometimes distress is caused by major stressors, and sometimes it is caused by too many minor stressors.

Minor stressors are things such as deadlines, long lines, heavy traffic, increasing gas prices, tight schedules, and not enough sleep or relaxation. Most of us carry accumulative effects of these everyday stressors, such as feeling tired and being mentally lethargic, unenthusiastic, and burdened. When these effects occur in my own life, I know it's time to simplify. I do this by planned neglect of something that, though it may be nice to do, is unnecessary (e.g., writing notes, making additional telephone calls). Also, I try to eliminate late-night television and get seven or more hours of sleep.

Like the barnacles on a ship, everyday stressors can sink our ship unless we manage them. Yet most of us merely try to cope, which can get old! Several years ago, the *Wall Street Journal* told of a corporate executive in New York City who gave up a six-figure salary for a lower-paying job in a small, upstate town. When asked why, he replied, "I have coped and coped until I have run out of cope." To live effectively as Christians, we need to be aware of the accumulative effects of everyday stressors and minimize them as much as possible.

Then there are major stressors, such as the death of a loved one, a divorce, the loss of a job, a serious illness, the rebellion of a child, or financial losses. Though minor stressors take their toll, major stressors can be devastating.

If you have ever had your life turned upside down by one of these major stressors, you know that you feel disoriented, as if a rug has been pulled out from under your feet. The accumulative effects of everyday stress are magnified, and we often feel panicked, have a desire to withdraw, and lose interest in activities that have been meaningful to us.

I talked with a man in his forties who had recently lost his wife. He was struggling alternately between feeling confident that he can make it and, the next day, feeling totally devastated. He wisely has gone back to work—work for the hands to do helps to heal a broken heart. He also continues to attend Sunday school and church as well as a support group. I suggested that it takes a full year to go through holidays, birthdays, and anniversaries before someone who is grieving feels somewhat normal again. In the meantime, it is important to eat nutritionally, exercise, and take time daily for honest conversation with God (which sometimes is easier to do through journaling), Bible reading, and silence.

Times of loss and illness and turmoil are times when our faith needs reinforcement. Unless we are proactive in dealing with major stressors such as these, we can find ourselves in a physical, mental, or spiritual meltdown. We can become physically ill, mentally unbalanced, spiritually parched, or a combination of these. After all, we are one entity—body, mind, and spirit. What happens in one area will affect the others. Unless we are integrated at the core through the commitment of our lives to Christ, we won't be able to see God's bigger picture. When major stressors come into our lives, we need to follow the advice of Gracie Allen, who said, "Don't put a period where God put a comma."

If you are experiencing a major stressor in your life, it is wise not to take on another stress-inducing activity at this time unless absolutely necessary, whether it be good or bad—such as moving, taking a new job, or having a confrontation with a friend. Remember that an accumulation of everyday stressors—even if many of them are motivating and helpful—can dilute our joy and color our lives gray. Add to that a major stressor, and we find ourselves in a continual cycle of worry and anxiety.

Let's look at some of the common causes of our stress and see how we can deal effectively with them.

Common Causes of Stress

Worry and Anxiety

Worry is a perversion of the virtue of concern. The difference between worry and concern is graphic. Worry is like a broken record. Our thoughts return again and again to the groove of worry without ever moving on. Concern, on the other hand, is recognizing a problem, analyzing it, and, after careful thought and prayer, making an action plan to address it.

A good example of worry is my Aunt Vera, who was the posterchild for worry. She was a pessimist by nature and did nothing to overcome it. It made her a whiner and complainer. She was the only one of my mother's family who married a wealthy spouse, but there was no peace in that household. After her husband died suddenly (my brother said he was sure that Uncle Grover had had all he could take of gloom and doom) and her daughters were married, Aunt Vera came regularly for a lengthy visit to the family of each of her brothers and sisters. In our household, we dreaded that visit like the plague. Nothing suited Aunt Vera. We had to stop the clock from chiming because it kept her awake. She didn't want to go to the church picnic because people and germs would be there. After we would put her on the train to go home, we would celebrate our freedom.

In fairness, I believe that Aunt Vera felt concerned about some problems, but instead of doing something to make them better, she just thought and talked about them until complaining became a habit. She needed to change her thinking before it settled into the rut of complaining. Though she attended church regularly, she never allowed the joy of Christ to permeate her life. She needed to heed the words of Paul: "Let the same mind be in you that was in Christ Jesus" (Philippians 2:5).

Anxiety is different from worry. *The New World Dictionary of American English* describes anxiety as a state of unrest about what may happen, or a concern about a future event. There is an overall feeling of anxiety in the hearts of many Americans today as a result of tragedies such as 9/11—the day that planes were hijacked by terrorists and crashed into the World Trade Center, the Pentagon, and the Pennsylvania countryside—and hurricanes Rita and Katrina, which have been called the hurricanes of the century. Many are anxious about potential future terrorist attacks and natural disasters. They have a sense of unrest about the future. They are troubled and fearful. They have a feeling of powerlessness.

In the world in which we live, most of us have had feelings such as this at times. So, what can we do to overcome them? Let me suggest three simple steps we can take.

1. We must do what we can to prepare for the storms in our lives—whether they be physical, mental, emotional, or spiritual storms. We must be proactive, not reactive.
2. We must know that we are not powerless in the face of tragedy and disaster. We can do all things through Christ.
3. Most important, we must remember who and whose we are—and, as a result, we will want to live our lives in love and in service.

When I am feeling anxious, I like to recall the following scriptures until I grow calm in my spirit:

• Be still, and know that I am God (Psalm 46:10 KJV).

- Thou wilt keep him in perfect peace, whose mind is stayed on thee (Isaiah 26:3 KJV).
- Peace I leave with you, my peace I give unto you: not as the world giveth, give I unto you. Let not your heart be troubled, neither let it be afraid (John 14:27 KJV).

I also think of two pictures of peace I once saw. One was a very placid lake where there was not even a ripple on the water. The other, which represents most of our lives, was a bird resting peacefully in her nest in a tree that was being blown violently by a storm. Both pictures were titled "Peace."

Finally, I turn my worries into prayers. In his letter to the Philippians, the apostle Paul writes, "Do not worry about anything, but in everything by prayer and supplication with thanksgiving let your requests be made known to God. And the peace of God, which surpasses all understanding, will guard your hearts and your minds in Christ Jesus" (4:6-7). Like the Philippians, we have worries and anxieties about our jobs, our homes, our families, our communities, and our world. The apostle Paul says that we should make our requests known to God—but with thanksgiving. Thanksgiving opens our hearts to God's creative ideas, power, and presence. Ingratitude snaps them closed.

Once when I was feeling particularly anxious and stressful over a problem and had done all I knew to do about it, I decided to follow Paul's suggestion. For one month, I prayed only prayers of thanksgiving. During that month I did no pleading and made no special requests; I offered only gratitude. An amazing thing happened. I began to see the problem in a much broader and more balanced perspective because I wasn't focused solely on the problem. As a result, it wasn't nearly as threatening as I had thought. I felt at peace and began to see little things I could do to bring a solution to the difficulty. Slowly, almost imperceptibly, the problem was resolved.

Paul had learned this lesson in his own adventurous life for Christ. He passed his discovery on to the Philippians—and, through the Scriptures, to generation after generation of

Christians. This simple solution so impressed me that his advice has become my first and only course of action when I am worried or anxious.

Worry is a thought, and we can change our thoughts. If we are chronic worriers, we need to hear these other words of Paul to the Philippians: "Let the same mind be in you that was in Christ Jesus" (2:5). Think of the mind of Christ—calm, clear, and centered in the presence of the living God. Jesus trusted in the power of God. If we want peace in our lives, then we must trust in the goodness of our God.

Change

Another common cause of stress is change. Isn't it amazing how much stress change causes in our lives? Logically, change is as certain as taxes, but emotionally we often resist it. My only granddaughter will soon marry a wonderful young man. It will signal a change in all our relationships. Though I truly want Ellen to be happily married, I will miss the closeness that my husband and I have had with her through the years—her popping in for a snack or a meal, a shower after an athletic event, or a run in our nearby park. What it means is that I need to open my heart to include another person into the inner circle. That will take flexibility and trust.

I read the story of a little boy who had attended the graveside funeral service of an elderly neighbor. He had heard the minister say, "Dust to dust and ashes to ashes." Later he asked his mom, "Did the minister mean that we come from dust and go back to dust when we die?" His mother replied, "That's true of our physical bodies, but we get a new spiritual body when we die; and that body will live forever." Very somberly the child replied, "Well, there are a bunch of people under my bed either coming or going."

Whether we are coming or going, we all will experience changes and variations in our lives. Change is inevitable, and change produces stress. Some people respond to change by trying to be in control. Others feel defeated by it, thinking they are a helpless plaything of some vast, unconscious force. In the words of Pulitzer Prize winner Maurice Maeterlinck, "The beginning of wisdom is the acknowledgment of our creaturehood." The truth is that we *are* limited and finite; however, our security and peace are in the love of an eternal God who gives hope and power for this life, and the promise of salvation and eternal life in the world to come. Unfortunately, we often try to prop ourselves up with what we consider security in the present world: wealth, health, prestige or power, and pleasure. These props cannot hold us up! They will change with circumstances. The only absolute constant in our lives is the eternal God.

The following story illustrates God's constancy amid life's challenges. William Stidger was for many years professor of Homiletics at Boston University School of Theology. My husband, Ralph, tells wonderful stories of being in Stidger's class. Stidger told his students to keep their eyes and ears open in everyday living so that they might see the corollaries between their experiences and the gospel. Then they could "preach out of the overflow."

To illustrate his point, he told about an experience he had had as a student at Brown University in Providence, Rhode Island. Each morning on his way to classes, he walked by a skyscraper under construction. As the building rose higher and higher, the steel workers began to look like pygmies doing their treacherous job. One morning the thing that he feared might happen did happen. One of the steeljacks lost his footing and came hurtling to his death among the horrified onlookers. The foreman immediately signaled for the hoist and came to stand over the mangled body. Removing his hard hat he said, half aloud and half to himself, "I told him not to lean against the wind."

The student had heard something he didn't understand. After the ambulance had taken the body away and the crowd had dispersed, Stidger found the foreman and asked what he had meant by that remark. Bracing himself against the building, the foreman replied, "That man was new on the job, and I had warned him about leaning against the wind. He was from an inland city and didn't understand the treacherous power of the coastal wind. Here on the ground, you don't feel the power so much, but fifty stories up, the wind is blowing at quite a gale. The temptation is to brace yourself against it, but the veteran workers know that it can stop suddenly." The foreman wiped tears from his cheek as he concluded, "This morning every man on the job knew immediately when the wind stopped blowing, and that's when he fell."

Suddenly it occurred to Stidger that all of us are tempted to lean against the winds that can quit blowing suddenly—the winds of wealth, a good family name, good health, a good job, and pleasure. In his mind, the young theologian was already writing a sermon about the only secure wind that will hold us in all circumstances: the love of God delivered to us through Jesus Christ. When we are rooted and grounded in this love, we take the first step into abundant living described by Jesus in John 10:10.

Practical Ways to Manage Stress

Unfortunately, Christians are not exempt from stress. We need to learn, along with everyone else, some practical ways of managing it. The big difference will be that we are undergirded by faith so that we will handle it differently. I find the following things to be helpful:

1. Give Up the Blame Game

Blaming others uses the energy we need to be effective. A psychologist told me once that the only person who can't be helped in counseling is the one who won't take responsibility for his or her actions.

I know a woman who never learned to take responsibility for her finances. Having been seriously ill since childhood, she was made even more dependent when her parents would not make her take responsibility for her actions as a high school and college student. She never received an allowance and learned to live within it. She never had the experience of earning extra money through jobs like babysitting. She was never expected to have that responsibility.

Even after she graduated from college and entered the workforce, her parents still had to pull her financial chestnuts out of the fire. When she married, she expected the same treatment from her husband; but that arrangement didn't work, and the marriage ended after a few months.

When we never learn to act responsibly, for whatever reason, we are tempted to blame and judge others when things don't work out well. In the Sermon on the Mount, Jesus shared this wisdom: "Do not judge, so that you may not be judged. For with the judgment you make you will be judged, and the measure you give will be the measure you get. Why do you see the speck in your neighbor's eye, but do not notice the log in your own eye?" (Matthew 7:1–3). We must give up the blame game and accept responsibility for our decisions and actions.

2. Stay Physically Fit

Obesity seems to have reached epidemic proportions in our nation. We put enormous stress upon our bodies when we carry around extra weight. And carrying around extra weight, in turn, increases our stress! It's a vicious cycle. For most of us, maintaining a healthy weight is easier said than done. All my life I have fought a battle to keep my weight under control. The other day I read that brain cells come and go. We lose some while others are being born. *Yes*, I thought, *but fat cells stay around forever!* The only thing that has ever worked for me is this approach: If it tastes good, spit it out! Seriously, the only cure is to eat nutritionally, watch our caloric intake, and exercise regularly. We must keep those muscles moving!

A good example of the importance of eating nutritionally is found in the first chapter of the book of Daniel in the Old Testament. King Nebuchadnezzar of Babylon (now Iraq) besieged the city of Jerusalem and took many of its citizens into captivity. The king told his palace master to bring the brightest and best of these men to him. They would be trained in Babylonian history and customs and would serve in the king's court. Daniel and his three friends, Shadrack, Meshack, and Abednego, were four of those chosen. The first day of their training, they were brought rich food and wine served to the courtiers. Daniel requested that they be given only vegetables and water. The palace master was afraid to do that, thinking they might become ill. Daniel asked the master to give him a ten-day test. At the end of that time, the king found Daniel and his friends to be sharper in their minds and healthier in their bodies than those who consumed the rich food. So, even centuries ago, Daniel and his friends proved the importance of a healthy diet (See Daniel 1:1-17).

3. Don't Overspend

Just as there is an epidemic of obesity, there also is an epidemic of credit card debt. The minister who counseled Ralph and me before our marriage reminded us that whatever our salaries, we could live financially in heaven or hell. Heaven, he said, is when we spend fifty dollars less each month than we earn. Hell, on the other hand, is regularly spending fifty dollars more than we earn. He explained that the stress and anxiety that result from overspending can kill romance and negatively affect a marriage relationship. As the old adage goes, "When the wolf is at the door, the lovebird flies out the window."

The stress of overspending affects all of us negatively, whether we are married or not. Jesus told us the importance of using money responsibly when he told the parable of the talents. Reread the parable for yourself, found in Matthew 25:14-30, and prayerfully consider what God may be saying to you about how you manage—or fail to manage—your own finances.

4. Choose to Be Happy

Happiness is a choice, just as misery is a choice. In many of her speeches, speaker and author Barbara Johnson says, "Pain is inevitable, but misery is a choice." Despite our problems, we have unbelievable blessings, and we need to count them often. We have been given the incredible gift of life and the opportunity to live in the greatest country on the earth—otherwise, why would so many people want to come here? And as Christians, we have been given the twin gifts of salvation and eternal life. What gifts! Let's allow "the joy of the LORD [to be our] strength" (Nehemiah 8:10 NIV).

5. Don't Procrastinate

Reread chapter 4 on procrastination and begin to break your habit of sitting on the fence and putting off what should be done today. Remember this quotation by West African award-winning percussionist Babatunde Olatunji: "Yesterday is history; tomorrow is a mystery; today is a gift. That's why we call it 'the present.'"

6. Organize Your Day

Much stress results from chaos. Paul says to the Christians at Corinth: "All things should be done decently and in order" (1 Corinthians 14:40). Though Paul was talking about the use of spiritual gifts in worship, the same advice can be used for everyday living. If I allow dirty clothes to collect and my family has nothing clean to wear, everyone is stressed. If I have so much clutter on my desk, I may miss an important appointment or fail to reply to an invitation.

Once I read a tongue-in-cheek article entitled "Clutter's Last Stand," which suggested such practical things as handling mail in three piles—answer today, later decision, file. Everything else should be discarded immediately. As for closets, the author suggested that nothing should be hung up that needed cleaning or mending. Those simple suggestions have saved me much stress and confusion. One of the most helpful organizational tips I've used, however, is to plan my week on Sunday and outline each day the night before.

Other resources I have found helpful and recommend include *Ordering Your Private World* (Nelson Books, 2003) by Gordon MacDonald, and *Margins* (NavPress, 1992) by Richard Swenson.

7. Have a Trusted Friend with Whom You Can Talk

The Miracle of Dialogue (HarperSanFrancisco, 1993) by Reuel Howe helped me understand the value of talking things through with a trusted friend. Talking with a confidant enables you to feel understood without feeling judged, and to see the problem objectively. When we share together in this way, we are doing precisely what Paul tells the Christians of Galatia to do: "Bear one another's burdens, and in this way you will fulfill the law of Christ" (Galatians 6:2).

8. Stay Close to Jesus, Our Ultimate Friend

Spend time each day in his presence to listen, learn, and pray. The prayer of John Greenleaf Whittier never fails to calm my spirit and renew my mind:

> Drop thy still dews of quietness,
> till all our strivings cease;
> take from our souls the strain and stress,
>   and let our ordered lives confess
> the beauty of thy peace.
> ("Dear Lord and Father of Mankind," 1872)

There is an old hymn entitled "Take Your Burden to the Lord and Leave It There." That's excellent advice—but not always easy to follow. Many of us take them there, but pick them right back up. The only way it works is to allow Christ to live within us. When he fills us with his spirit, we are able to turn to him for guidance and then trust him for the future. Only then can the weight of stress drop from our shoulders.

There is no doubt about it: Ours is a world full of stress. We can use some of the practical steps listed in this chapter, but most of all, we can find peace in the midst of chaos when we have surrendered our lives to Christ.

Digging a Little Deeper

1. Is there someone with whom you currently are in conflict or from whom you are estranged? What steps can you take to seek reconciliation so that you may experience God's peace? Make your requests known to God in prayer with thanksgiving.

2. Describe someone you know who has dealt effectively with a major stressor such as the death of a loved one, divorce, financial disaster, or the betrayal of a friend. What, in your observation, are the resources that enabled this person to go through the experience so well?

3. What are some of the little, everyday stressors that can accumulate in our lives? What are some of the negative results they can cause? What or who really bugs you? How do you tend to cope with these stressors? Prayerfully consider the minor stressors in your life and determine how you might deal with them more effectively. Write a plan of action.

4. What are some of the things we tend to worry about? Read Philippians 4:6-7. Why is it important to make our request to God with thanksgiving?

5. At what point has change been stressful in your life? How did you deal with it? Do you wish you had done it differently? How?

6. Discuss the practical ways of managing stress (pp. 53–57). Which do you think you would find most helpful, and why? Choose one idea and begin applying it today.

Chapter 6

SLAYING THE GIANT OF PERFECTIONISM

Stand fast therefore in the liberty wherewith Christ hath made us free, and be not entangled again with the yoke of bondage.
(Galatians 5:1 KJV)

Once while speaking at a church in another state, I observed some of the most beautiful Renaissance religious art I have ever seen. "Where did you get that art?" I asked one of the church members in amazement. "These were painted by a man in our church," was the answer. Excitedly I said, "I want to meet that man," but nobody seemed thrilled about introducing him. As soon as I was introduced, I knew why. He was a perfectionist, and he expected everyone else to be, too.

Several of us were gathered to see and hear about his magnificent artwork, but he was preoccupied with telling us exactly where to stand so that the light would be perfect on each painting. One of the men had a very creative suggestion for the use of one painting, but it was not acceptable to the artist. The reason was not that he is a control freak or simply a bossy, overbearing man. Rather, he was unreceptive to the idea because whatever he does must be perfect, which includes the lighting and use of his artwork. He doesn't have the same attitude about the work of others, although he may become critical in the future if his perfectionism is left unchecked.

I was aware of this man's perfectionism because it takes one to know one. Years ago, I fought the giant of perfectionism. In fact, I can remember almost having an anxiety attack when I didn't have time to polish my children's shoes for Sunday school and church. That's bondage, not freedom or excellence. *But aren't we supposed to strive for excellence and Christian perfection?* you may be wondering. Absolutely! But this means to grow more and more into the likeness of Christ. Perfectionism, on the other hand, is a counterfeit of both. So, we must strive for excellence, not perfection—remembering that perfectionism is *not* a twenty-first century phenomenon.

Elijah Was a Perfectionist

Even as early as 850 BC, there were perfectionists. The prophet Elijah had many of the characteristics of a perfectionist. He had a sensitive, somewhat melancholic personality; he wanted to do things well, and when he didn't, he easily fell into self-pity and depression. He was totally committed to Yahweh, the God of Abraham, Isaac, Jacob, and Moses. A powerful prophet of this faith, he was deeply disturbed when King Ahab had allowed his foreign wife, Jezebel, to set up shrines for her foreign gods.

God asked Elijah to confront Ahab and tell him that there would be no rain until he, Elijah, gave the word. After the confrontation, Elijah disappeared for three years, during which time the drought worsened and Ahab looked in vain for the prophet. Finally, God instructed Elijah to present himself to the king.

Elijah asked that all the people of Israel appear on Mount Carmel—with the priests of Baal on one side and Elijah, the lone prophet of Yahweh, on the other. There were two altars ready for sacrifice. It was agreed that the god who lighted the fire on the altar would be worshiped in Israel. The priests of Baal went first, pleading with their god to send down fire. They were there all day and into the evening, but no fire. Then Elijah instructed men to pour four barrels of water over the altar at three different times. The altar was soaked, but when Elijah prayed to Yahweh, fire like a lightening bolt descended and consumed the sacrifice; and the people of Israel cheered. It was a great victory for God and Elijah! But when Jezebel learned that all of her prophets had been killed, she sent word to Elijah that he would be killed that day.

In the true nature of a perfectionist, Elijah was unhappy and upset that not everyone was pleased with his performance. He sat under a juniper tree and felt sorry for himself. Finally, God's voice came to Elijah—not in the wind, or the earthquake, or the fire, but in a still, small voice. God told Elijah to be done with his fear, to get to work again, and to trust God for the future. (See the full story in 1 Kings 18:19.)

Like Elijah, we often struggle with perfectionism and feel sorry for ourselves when things don't go as we think they should. Let's take a closer look at this giant called perfectionism.

What Is Perfectionism?

For me, it was David Seamands who shone the light of truth on the malady of perfectionism as I read his book *Healing for Damaged Emotions* (Chariot Victor Press, 1981). In the book he quotes psychologist Karen Horney: "Perfectionism is the tyranny of the ought's (hardening of the oughteries). It is a feeling of never doing well enough or being good enough." Seamands suggests that included among the causes of perfectionism are certain temperaments, overly strict parents, dysfunction in the home, or a combination of these causes.

In retrospect, I think my own tendency toward perfectionism came from the alcoholism of my dad and the negativism of my mother, leaving me with a low self-image. That, combined with a strong inner desire to achieve, left me feeling that I could never measure up to what I wanted to be. Two things helped me over a long period of time. First, my commitment to Christ allowed me to relax and trust God's future for me as I internalized God's unconditional love. Second, some of my accomplishments enabled me to see that others perceived me as a leader. Even so, it has taken me a long time to accept and believe in myself.

Perfectionism often begins with self-deprecation. There is a definite connection between low self-esteem and performance. Interestingly, some people with low self-esteem have learned to compensate by appearing to be extremely confident, self-assured, and even arrogant. Yet, when their actions are questioned or their projects don't turn out well, they become angry or crash into self-pity. Their outward confidence has been a charade, and their low self-esteem continues to haunt them.

The symptoms of perfectionism, according to Seamands, include anxiety, an overly sensitive conscience under a giant umbrella of guilt, anxiety, condemnation, and legalism—an emphasis on the dos and don'ts. Perfectionists often display a tender conscience, a low self-esteem, and an automatic guilt that is extremely sensitive to what others think of them. Seamands writes: "The do's and don'ts keep piling up because they have more and more people to please, so the halo has to be adjusted so often it becomes what Paul calls 'a yoke of bondage.'" And this yoke of bondage can have damaging results.

The Results of Perfectionism

Among the results of perfectionism is the need to be a people pleaser. When I became a minister's wife, I wanted to be the perfect minister's wife. It didn't take me long to realize that there wasn't just one image of the perfect minister's wife; there were as many images as there were members! The second most freeing day for me was when I could say, "Lord, I want to be the finest person I can be for you, but I'm not going to 'play to the grandstand' any longer."

Anger is another common byproduct of perfectionism. Often this anger stems from resentment—resentment against the "ought's," resentment against ourselves for not being all we would like to be, or even resentment against God. The latter is not anger against the loving, gracious, self-giving God who comes to us through Christ, but anger against a caricature of a God who is never satisfied. If this anger continues over a period of time, one of three things will likely happen: a breakaway from faith, an emotional breakdown, or a breakthrough to freedom.

Years ago we had a neighbor who had pulled away from faith because he thought God had called him into the ministry and he had not answered the call. God wasn't condemning the man. Rather, his own perfectionistic tendencies were condemning him. When the man would drink, which became increasingly often, he would come to our house and pour out the story again and again. We assured him that God loved him unconditionally, and that God had called all of us to be ministers, though not necessarily ordained clergy. We emphasized that he could serve God in the business world or wherever he was. Yet his perfectionism would not allow him to accept anything less than his perfect picture of what he should be. In the meantime, he stayed away from church and his drinking increased.

While writing this chapter, I received a telephone call from a friend whose feelings of self-condemnation for her perceived inability to please others have landed her in a psychiatric hospital. Trudy said that she felt as if she were in a swimming pool trying to keep multiple beach balls submerged. There are so many of them that one or two keep popping up above the surface. She is in no sense delusional, nor is she unable to reason. Rather, she is in an emotional meltdown because of a very low self-esteem that has hardened into perfectionism.

How, then, can we become free from perfectionism?

Freedom from Perfectionism and Performance-Based Acceptance

Seamands reminds us that the good news is not the path of perfect performance. We cannot win God's favor. Rather, God's favor is the gift of God's grace—a freely given, undeserved, nonrepayable favor. God's loving acceptance has nothing to do with our worthiness. Our acceptance is based not on what we have done but on what God has done for us through Christ. Still, a gift is not a gift until we receive it. When we truly accept the priceless gift of God's love and internalize it, we become a whole new person—free at last.

The apostle Paul explained this succinctly in Ephesians 2:8-9: "For by grace you have been saved through faith, and this is not your own doing; it is the gift of God—not the result of works, so that no one may boast." Still, in our culture we often judge others by their performance. Let's remember as parents and grandparents that we need to affirm children for who they are, motivate them to use all their gifts, rejoice in their achievements, and *never* compare them with others. Never by our words, actions, or facial expressions should we indicate that we consider them a failure.

For me, freedom from perfectionism and performance-based acceptance has meant an inner healing and reprogramming. Keeping a journal of my honest feelings has helped me live out my freedom, as well as reading good books, listening to tapes, learning biblical affirmations, and spending time in positive prayer and with positive, joyful people. Of course, I am still very much a Christian under construction. God hasn't finished with me yet. So, whenever I get discouraged with my thoughts or actions, I reread Philippians 1:6: "Being confident of this, that he who began a good work in you will carry it on to completion until the day of Christ Jesus" (NIV). God is still working out his plan in each one of us. To God be the glory! Our responsibility is not to seek perfection, but to "seek first the kingdom of God and His righteousness" (Matthew 6:33 NKJV) in order that we may become, through the grace of God, the love of Christ and the empowerment of the Holy Spirit—all that we were created to be.

Though it is often difficult for us to accept and believe, we have already been set free. When writing to the Christians in Galatia, Paul said: "Stand fast therefore in the liberty wherewith Christ hath made us free, and be not entangled again with the yoke of bondage" (Galatians 5:1 KJV). Paul was writing to people who once had understood that we are set free through Christ's death on the cross, but they now were backsliding into the belief that salvation comes through the "dos and don'ts" of the Jewish law. He was saying, in effect, that it is the love of Christ that constrains us. We cannot ruin a life that God paid for with his own life. We are free, yet our freedom gives us the desire and ability to love our neighbor as ourselves. We stand firm, then, in the freedom that Christ has given us to love God and neighbor.

The fact that our freedom has already been bought for us by Christ is a foundation stone of the Christian gospel. Our part comes in seeking to fulfill God's purpose for our lives. Even though we know we can do nothing without Christ (John 15:5), we also know that "with God all things are possible" (Matthew 19:26 NIV). I like to compare this to having a beautiful flower garden. God has created the soil, the sun, and the rain—all essential for growing flowers. Yet, weeds will grow in that garden unless we plant flower seeds and cultivate the garden. It is a joint venture. Without God, there would be no garden; without us, the flowers would not grow. What a great way to use our God-given abilities and trust God for the outcome.

Overcoming the Giant of Perfectionism

Although our freedom has been won by Christ, there are still things that we can do to affirm and use that freedom. Some of these include the following:

1. Recognize the symptoms of perfectionism, such as low self-esteem, anxiety, an overly sensitive conscience, guilt, condemnation, and legalism. I know the symptoms because I was a perfectionist, and occasionally when I am unusually tired, I revert to the old pattern. But I know that Christ can set us free, so I try always to change with his help. You, too, can determine to change with the help of Christ.

   Note: Don't do the following two exercises on the same day. It is so easy to focus on our weaknesses rather than to build on our strengths. Take time to recognize and celebrate your strengths first.

2. Sit down alone in a quiet place and make a list of your assets or strengths. This list can include things such as a healthy body and a good mind, but it also should focus on your unique talents—such as friendliness or a talent for singing, speaking,

playing a musical instrument, writing, cooking, organization, and so on. Take time to give God thanks for each of these gifts and to celebrate them.

3. Sit down alone and quietly make a list of things you wish to change or improve in order to be the person you were created to be. This list might include things such as improving your health and physical fitness, exercising regularly, eating nutritionally, learning to relax, losing weight, learning new skills, giving up a destructive habit or bad attitude, building relationships with significant others in your life, settling your past, or taking time to grow spiritually.

4. Choose *one* of your weaknesses and make an action plan to work on it for one week. For example, if you choose to lose weight and become more physically fit, you can make an appointment at a weight reduction center and/or an exercise program. Or you can decide to watch your fat intake, give up dessert each day, and walk fifteen to thirty minutes each day. Write down your plan and follow it. Make faith and prayer important parts of your action plan.

5. As you begin to get mastery over one area, begin to work on another; but always keep balance and perspective. Remember that we are Christians under construction, and that there is no instant wholeness. God's sanctifying grace is at work in us. Our job is to cooperate with him, to live in fellowship with Christ, and to know that "[the One] who began a good work in you will carry it on to completion" (Philippians 1:6 NIV).

6. Stop beating yourself up when you have fallen short. Arnold Palmer says that when he makes a bad golf shot, he says, "Next time, I'll put it on the green," and he visualizes the shot and follow through. He never mentally replays a bad shot or beats himself up about it. Likewise, we shouldn't replay our mistakes and see ourselves as failures. Rather, we must remind ourselves that

God is at work within us and that "he who began a good work in you will carry it on to completion until the day of Christ Jesus." Stop trying to do everything in your own strength.

7. Discover the power of affirmations. In my own life, I have used affirmations, particularly biblical affirmations, to condition my mind and spirit. I recommend the following to enable you to build self-esteem and to empower you to live the abundant life.

Affirmations to Improve Self-Esteem

The following affirmations—some are scripture verses and some are positive statements—have helped me tremendously as I have sought to move from a negative, pessimistic self-image to a confident self-image that encourages me to grow in competence and become what God is calling me to be.

Say at least one of the following affirmations when you first awaken. These affirmations also may be used anytime when you feel inferior or inadequate or pressured to perform.

1. I am created in the image of God, redeemed by Jesus Christ, and empowered by the Holy Spirit.
2. "I can do all things through Christ who strengthens me" (Philippians 4:13 NKJV).
3. "If God be for us, who can be against us?" (Romans 8:31 KJV).
4. I am a Christian under construction. God hasn't finished with me yet.
5. "[The one] who began a good work in you will carry it on to completion" (Philippians 1:6 NIV).
6. I am unique. I like myself and enjoy being me.
7. Today I will treat everyone with whom I come in contact (including myself) with respect and appreciation.
8. I am capable and confident. I will remember to look people in the eye. I know that direct eye contact when speaking or listening is one of the most important nonverbal indicators of self-confidence.

9. I enjoy smiling, and I smile frequently. A smile communicates in every language one's acceptance of self and others.
10. "This is the day the LORD has made; let us rejoice and be glad in it" (Psalm 118:24 NIV).

The purpose of affirmations is never to glorify ourselves because we remember that without Christ, we can do nothing. (John 15:5). Throughout the Old and New Testaments we are told to walk in humility so that in our weaknesses Christ's power can be seen. Among those scriptures is this verse: "And what does the LORD require of you but to do justice, and to love kindness, and to walk humbly with your God" (Micah 6:8).

The apostle Paul prayed three times to have his thorn in the flesh removed, and it was not. When God reminded him, "My grace is sufficient for you, for power is made perfect in weakness," Paul said, "So I will boast all the more gladly of my weaknesses, so that the power of Christ may dwell in me. . . . Whenever I am weak, then I am strong" (2 Corinthians 12:9). May we do the same!

Digging a Little Deeper

1. How would you define perfectionism? What are some of the signs or symptoms of perfectionism? What are some of the results? (Refer to pp. 61–62, "What Is Perfectionism?")
2. Are you caught in the bondage of perfectionism in any area of your life? Explain.
3. Reread Galatians 5:1-5 *as a group.* In verse 1, Paul says that he isn't sent by human authority. Who does he think sent him? What did Christ do to set us free? (See verse 4.) Give thanks for your freedom.
4. What is "performance-based acceptance"? Give several examples. Read Ephesians 2:8-9. According to the apostle Paul, what saves us and sets us free? What should be our motivation for doing good works? Why is performance-based acceptance a perversion of the gospel?

5. How might keeping a journal help you overcome perfectionism? How can inspirational books and tapes and biblical affirmations help you overcome perfectionism?
6. Name one practical thing you can begin doing today that will enable God to break a tendency you may have toward perfectionism in any area of your life.

Chapter 7

SLAYING THE TWIN GIANTS
OF ANGER AND RESENTMENT

*Saul threw his spear at him to strike him; so Jonathan knew
that it was the decision of his father to put David to death.*
(1 Samuel 20:33)

Is everybody in the world angry? I wondered as I witnessed some
bona fide road rage on the interstate. The woman driving ahead of
me was thrown into a rage when a young man cut sharply in front
of her from another lane. It's true that she had to brake momentarily, but her angry reaction almost caused an interstate pile-up.
When she came to a sudden stop, while wildly blowing her horn
and yelling out of an open window, you could hear brakes squeal-
ing for some distance.

Even that didn't satisfy her. The young man who provoked her
wrath sped away in an obvious attempt to escape her rage. But she
gave chase and soon was right behind him, flashing her lights and
blowing her horn. Fortunately my exit came up shortly, but I had
hardly recovered when I encountered another incident. In the
drugstore parking lot, a man was loudly and angrily berating his
ten-year-old son, who obviously paid more for an item than his
father approved. Granted, it was an issue that needed to be
addressed, but not in a public parking lot, and not with such
anger.

These incidents make me wonder what is happening to civility
and cause me to think of the devastation in lives when anger is
uncontrolled. Feeling angry is not wrong. Anger actually tells us
that something is amiss. Only when anger is uncontrolled and

expressed destructively does it destroy friendships, marriages, organizations, and even nations. This kind of out-of-control anger, unfortunately, is nothing new.

Uncontrolled Anger Is Not a New Phenomenon

One of the best examples of uncontrolled anger and its consequences can be found in 1 Samuel 18-20. Saul's anger against David was irrational and uncontrolled. Though Saul was grateful to David for slaying Goliath, the king became jealous of the handsome young warrior as he returned from fighting the Philistines and the women were singing and dancing in the streets, saying: "Saul has killed his thousands, and David his ten thousands" (1 Samuel 18:7). Unchecked anger only grows, which is why we later see the king becoming furious with his son, Jonathan, for befriending David (20:33).

As pre-arranged, David was in hiding, and Jonathan took a bow with him and shot arrows beyond David to signal that David's life was in jeopardy and that he should move on. Saul's anger hardened into deep resentment, and he spent the rest of his life pursuing the young warrior. Though David had several opportunities to retaliate, he never did. Unlike Saul, he was able to handle his anger in constructive ways, writing some of the most beautiful, heartfelt psalms that have comforted and blessed us all.

Saul's life was full of torment because of his uncontrolled, angry pursuit of David. After several unsuccessful attempts to kill David, Saul went to battle against the Philistines. In the battle, all of Saul's sons, including Jonathan, were killed. Realizing that the battle was lost, Saul asked his honor bearer to use his sword and kill the king. The armor bearer was afraid and refused to do it, so Saul—lonely, angry, and afraid—took his own life.

When David learned this, he mourned for the king and his son Jonathan. He learned that some men of Jabesh-Gilead had found Saul's body and had buried it. David invoked the blessing of the Lord upon him. Returning to his home country, of the tribe of Judah, in the city of Hebron, he was anointed king as Samuel had prophesied. Though there was some resistance from Saul's followers from the north, David eventually united the country and became Israel's greatest king. Despite some big mistakes in his life, David stayed close to God.

Anger Can Be Used for Good

Anger is much like steam—it can be used to blow a horn, making a loud noise, or it can be used to move a steamship toward its destination. We can become angry over little things, such as when we are inconvenienced or when our feelings have been hurt. On the other hand, we can right a terrible wrong when anger is channeled into constructive action.

For example, when Abraham Lincoln reportedly witnessed a young black woman being pulled away from her husband and child and sold into slavery, he said with anger in his voice, "This is wrong, and if I ever have a chance to hit it, I'll hit it hard." Years later when he became president of the United States, he did just that. The result was the Emancipation Proclamation, which he issued on January 1, 1863.

Vernon Johns, a civil rights pioneer, was a man whose anger over segregation caused him to move in small but powerful ways to change the situation. When he was pastor of Dexter Avenue Baptist Church in Montgomery, Alabama, his organist was a young woman named Rosa Parks. Johns often used his sermons to empower the African American congregation to stand courageously against injustice and moral wrongs. When the controversy over his preaching cost him his church, his successor, Martin Luther King Jr., inherited a congregation willing to stand up for their beliefs, and the result changed our nation forever.

All of us should feel enough anger over certain evils that we want to do something to correct them. An example of this is the organization MADD, which was formed by mothers whose children were killed by drunk drivers. The name of the organization is an acronym for Mothers Against Drunk Driving. They have secured legislation for stricter laws and sentences against drunk driving.

Others use their anger to fight against cancer and other diseases, drug abuse, missing children, child pornography, and child abuse. We all are called to use our anger to fight against evil, rather than allow our anger to harden into resentment.

Anger Hardens into Resentment

When we refuse to use our anger for good and choose instead to allow it to fester, it hardens into resentment. Resentment is like a splinter under the skin. If it is not removed, it causes infection in a personality.

In 2005, newspapers and TV news broadcasts reported that Judge Joan Lefkow of Chicago returned to her home after a day on the bench to find her husband, Michael, a sixty-four-year-old attorney, and her eighty-nine-year-old mother, Donna, lying in pools of blood. Both had been shot at close range. The newspaper accounts described the judge's anguish when she said, "If someone hated me, they should kill me instead of my family."

Later reports indicated that when the assailant learned that the judge wasn't at home, he shot the two people who were present. The murderer was not a white supremacist as was first believed, but one who was consumed with hatred and resentment over a mouth cancer that had left him disfigured. He had sued the doctor, the hospital, the lawyer, the judge, and others. Unsuccessful at each of these attempts, he picked up a gun—determined to kill someone. When he was stopped at a road-check, he killed himself. His suicide note gave a full description of what he had been through and how his anger had hardened into resentment and, finally, murder.

Another vivid example of anger hardening into resentment is seen in the story of a beautiful woman in her fifties who found herself in the hospital because her body could assimilate no food. Everything she ate was rejected by her system. This had happened over such a long period of time that she was actually dying. After a series of tests indicated no physical reason for this rejection of food, the doctor called her minister to see if he could detect some emotional reason for the malady.

When the minister called on the woman in the hospital, he explained the seriousness of her situation and asked if she were troubled by something in her family life. Amid sobs, the woman explained that her husband had had a brief affair with a neighbor when they had moved to another city. Though it had happened years earlier and she had forgiven her husband, she had not forgiven the other woman who had been involved. Her long-held resentment had resulted in her body's rejection of food. In fact, she even admitted in a bitter outburst of tears, "I could tear her limb from limb."

The minister gave her some books to read that described the marked effects of resentment. When she fully understood that her resentment was about to take her life, she surrendered the wrong and found forgiveness through prayer. Soon thereafter, she was back in church with a radiant face, waving to her doctor sitting in his pew. He described her recovery as a miracle. Indeed, it was a miracle of God's grace!

Doctors in the field of psychiatry have called resentment one of the most virulent germs that can attack the human mind. It is especially dangerous because so often it does its deadly work without being isolated. That is, it is not recognized for what it is. When resentment begins to work, it breeds bitterness, depression, and disease. It causes nervous breakdowns and mental unbalance and kills joy. Resentment also fosters self-pity, because some people feel that their resentment is justified. Yet, whether justified or not, the destructive results of resentment are the same.

When we refuse to use our anger for good but allow it to harden into resentment, we create havoc for ourselves and for others. I know a woman whose brother said something unkind to her at a family gathering twenty-six years ago. Though he called to apologize, she would not talk with him, and her resentment has grown through the years. When their parents were killed, they both were at the memorial service, but there was no communication between them. Her resentment has denied her children of knowing their cousins, of attending family reunions, and of having a happy mom.

There have been times when she needed her only sibling to share her pain, but resentment kept her from letting him know. She thinks she is punishing him for an unkind remark, but she has made herself an angry, bitter woman; and her attitude has produced conflict in her own family. Think how forgiveness could change that picture. It's no wonder that Jesus told Peter to forgive a person seventy times seven—in other words, more times than we can count.

People who allow resentment to turn into bitterness, hatred, or depression actually self-destruct. They may continue to function, but inside they have lost peace of mind, hope, and happiness. Long-held resentment may even turn to revenge

Resentment Often Leads to Revenge

The definition of *revenge* in the *New World Dictionary of American English* is "to inflict damage, injury, or punishment in return for an insult or injury; to avenge." Sadly, revenge is encouraged in many ways in our culture today. Even bumper stickers promote revenge with sayings such as, "Don't get mad; get even." Revenge and violence are encouraged in popular songs, movies, and TV sit coms, dramas, and talk shows. For many people, revenge has become a way of life—an expected reaction. We see it lived out in gang violence and vendetta killings, school killings, random drive-by shootings, and domestic violence.

In small or large towns where people seem civil, even neighborly, there are examples of less violent forms of revenge. A friend told me recently of a man in her neighborhood who has a beautiful yard but who gives unsolicited advice to neighbors about theirs. Many in the neighborhood appreciate and follow his advice. One man, however, completely ignored it. Now, the giver of advice won't allow his wife to invite the other family to their annual open house. This is the third year of the revenge tactic, and neighbors are taking sides.

A girl in one of our local high schools was blackballed from membership in a social group by a girl who was jealous. The girl who was blackballed is a beautiful, loving Christian girl who had never experienced rejection in such a flagrant manner. She was devastated, and it took a long time to restore her trust level again. Inadvertently, the perpetrator admitted what she had done to another member. Soon she was feeling rejection from the group. It was a chaotic scene that could have been avoided.

I must admit that I laughed heartily over one story of revenge that seemed to be more representative of creative thinking than personal revenge. This story is probably an urban legend since it came to me via the Internet from a friend. It is entitled "The Dress."

Jennifer's wedding day was fast approaching. Nothing could dampen her excitement—not even her parent's nasty divorce. Her mother had found the perfect dress to wear—the perfect dress to be the best-dressed mother of the bride ever!

A week later, Jennifer was horrified to learn that her father's new young wife had bought the exact same dress. Jennifer asked the new wife to exchange it, but she refused. "Absolutely not. I look like a million bucks in this dress and I'm wearing it," she replied.

Jennifer told her mother, who graciously said, "Never mind, sweetheart. I'll get another dress. After all, it's your special day." A few days later, they went shopping and did find another beautiful dress. When they stopped for lunch, Jennifer asked her mother, "Aren't you going to return the other dress? You really don't have another occasion to wear it."

The mother just smiled and replied, "Of course I do, dear. I'm wearing it to the rehearsal dinner the night before the wedding!"

Though this is a humorous story, even seemingly harmless examples of revenge cause damage to relationships. Revenge begets revenge, and the cycle produces endless conflict and strife where peace could abide. God wants our hearts to remain pure so that Christ can live within us to bring joy, peace, and love.

In our angry, vengeful society, we need to heed Paul's words to the Romans: "If it is possible, so far as it depends on you, live peaceably with all. Beloved, never avenge yourselves, but leave room for the wrath of God; for it is written, 'Vengeance is mine, I will repay, says the Lord'" (Romans 12:18-19).

How to Overcome Resentment

Overcoming resentment is not easy, but the following things have helped me:

1. Work on Your Anger Before Resentment Develops

Anger is a thought, and a thought can be changed. At a conference I once attended, I heard James Mallory, a Christian psychiatrist and author of *The Kink and I*, speak on anger. He said that we have twenty seconds between becoming aware of our anger and choosing our reaction. He encouraged us to use these twenty seconds to breathe deeply and pray for guidance. Just a few seconds will allow us to temper our reaction so that we may decide later on a constructive plan of action.

To illustrate his point, he told of an incident in his own family. One Sunday, he and his wife and their four children were getting dressed for Sunday school and church. He overheard his wife say to Terry, their four-year-old son, "Hurry up and get dressed for Sunday school." The little guy was trying, but he couldn't find his socks; and that jammed his "computer," so he just sat down.

On her next "hurry up" run through the room, the mother told Terry that his socks were in the room of his teenage brother, Jimmy. Mallory came down the hall and heard Jimmy, who knew that his little brother often messed up his room, say to the four-year-old, "You are not coming in here." Realizing that Terry was caught between the "hurry up" of his mother downstairs and the "You're not coming in here" of his brother upstairs, Mallory became furious. He said that he rushed to Jimmy's room, pushed the fifteen-year-old onto the bed, and shouted, "Why don't you act like a Christian?"

He said that it took the family all day to get over that incident. After he apologized to Jimmy, he realized that if he had used the twenty seconds to think calmly and prayerfully, things could have been different. He said, "All I had to do was to go to Jimmy's room and say calmly, 'Move over Jimmy; your brother needs his socks.'" The incident could have been avoided if he hadn't reacted instantly.

In my own life, I remember, as if a neon sign were calling my attention to it, the day I lost control with one of my children. It was a minor misdemeanor, but one that had caused me great inconvenience. As I said some harsh, unkind words, I suddenly saw the look of deep hurt in my son's eyes. I stopped in midsentence, asked for forgiveness for my explosion, and explained why the misdemeanor must not be repeated. Then I made a hasty retreat to my bedroom where I dropped to my knees and asked God for forgiveness and for help in controlling my anger.

In my own case, I began to see other destructive patterns that fed my anger and needed to be dealt with for my own spiritual and emotional health, as well as for my relationships. Patterns such as perfectionism, self-centeredness, and paralyzing fear began to surface. Even the source of some of my pent-up rage became evident—my father's alcoholism at a very vulnerable time in my life.

Obviously, all of this didn't happen in one session with God. My desire and decision to change were reinforced by an honest look at my life and relationships, a disciplined prayer life in which I sought guidance, wide reading in the area of Christian living, and the practice of keeping a spiritual journal. These are some of the ways we can stay in touch with our spiritual core in a noisy, fast-paced, technological world.

The New Testament shows us how Jesus handled anger and resentment. In the Sermon on the Mount, Jesus advised his followers to "settle matters quickly with your adversary" (Matthew 5:25 NIV). He seemed to be saying that we shouldn't harbor anger and allow it to fester. We shouldn't focus on it because, as the saying goes, "what gets your attention gets you." Rather, we should seek reconciliation as soon as possible.

2. Seek Reconciliation

Earlier in the Sermon on the Mount, Jesus said, "So when you are offering your gift at the altar, if you remember that your brother or sister has something against you, leave your gift there before the altar and go; first be reconciled to your brother or sister, and then come and offer your gift" (Matthew 5:23-24).

How wonderful it would be if all misunderstandings and conflicts could be quickly resolved. When we've been hurt, rejected, or treated unfairly, we usually don't want to forgive. Reconciliation is the last thing on our minds. What do we do, then? I suggest five things:

1. Take a little time to think through what actually caused the incident. Were you guilty of triggering it?
2. Talk it over with a trusted Christian friend to get a clearer perspective.
3. Remember how many times God has forgiven you. Ask God for willingness to offer forgiveness.
4. Act! First, forgive the person in your heart. Then, stay open to the possibility of reconciliation (even if this is not what you want). You will feel a great weight lifted off your shoulders.
5. Give thanks to God for his faithfulness.

In his book *Forgive and Forget* (Simon and Schuster, 1984), Lewis B. Sneeds says, "Forgiveness is God's invention for coming to terms with the world in which, despite their best intentions, people are unfair to each other and hurt each other deeply. God began by forgiving us and invites us to forgive each other."

Most important, by his words and actions Jesus illustrated that forgiveness is the authentic way to overcome resentment. In Matthew 18:21, Peter asks the Lord, "Lord, if another member of the church sins against me, how often should I forgive? As many as seven times?" The Jewish law required that you forgive your enemy three times. So, Peter thought he was being especially gracious when he suggested seven times. Jesus said to Peter, "Not seven times but seventy-seven times." In other words, we shouldn't even keep count of how often we forgive. Forgiveness should be our lifestyle. I'm convinced that Jesus knew that when we refuse to forgive a person, we are tied to that person. Their actions determine our reactions.

When one of the disciples asked Jesus to teach them to pray, he gave them the words we now call the "Lord's Prayer." In this prayer is the phrase "forgive us our sins, for we ourselves forgive everyone indebted to us" (Luke 11:4). Of course, the greatest example of forgiveness Jesus gave us was when he was hanging in agony on the cross with nails piercing his hands and feet. He said, "Father, forgive them; for they do not know what they are doing" (Luke 23:34).

All of these words of Jesus were very real to me when I heard E. Stanley Jones, who was a missionary to India and an evangelist to America, tell the story of an Armenian girl and her brother who had been attacked by a Turkish soldier. She was able to escape, but her brother was shot and killed. Later the girl became a nurse. One day that Turkish soldier was brought into the ward of the hospital in which she worked. She recognized him immediately as the one who had brutally murdered her brother. Immediately she felt anger and wanted revenge. The soldier was critically ill, even hanging between life and death. His life was in her hands. The slightest neglect and he would die. As she prayed about this matter, she knew that revenge was not the answer. Instead, through the power of Christ, she forgave the soldier, fought for his life, and nursed him back to health.

One day when he was convalescing, she told him who she was. The soldier looked at her in astonishment and asked, "Why didn't you let me die when I was in your power?" She replied, "I couldn't because I am a Christian, and Christ forgave even the people who crucified him. Through his power, I can do the same."

I'm convinced that this is impossible unless we live in daily relationship with the One who removes our sins from us "as far as the east is from the west." Even so, reconciliation is difficult even when both persons really want it. What if the other person rejects your offer?

Let's suppose that you've done everything you can to effect reconciliation. You've extended forgiveness and/or asked for forgiveness for whatever misunderstanding may have occurred—even though it may have been unintentional or inadvertent on either or both of your parts. You also have expressed your sincere desire to restore the relationship. The other person slams the door shut. What then? There are four things that can help.

- Release the problem to God and leave it there.
- Don't allow the action of your adversary to determine how you will react.
- Don't keep it alive by focusing on it or talking with others about it.
- Stay open to the possibility of reconciliation initiated by the other person.

Let's remember that our job is to give honest forgiveness and the offer of reconciliation. Then the ball is in the other person's court! Even Jesus, after having forgiven Caiaphas, Pontius Pilate, and the Roman soldiers, didn't rush after them begging for reconciliation.

3. If Necessary, Allow Restorative Waiting

God's time is not our time. Though restorative waiting is often hard, it is sometimes necessary to fulfill God's purposes.

For example, let's say that two people are thoroughly and justifiably angered by the sneering arrogance of a third person. Neither of the two responds immediately, but there is a striking difference in their waiting. One is simply holding in the rage and sowing the seedbed of resentment. The other has relaxed into what might be called restorative waiting. He is giving his ego time to heal from the hurt he has suffered and time to prepare for a constructive response.

As we look at the life story of David—from his teenage slaying of Goliath to his ascendancy to king of Israel—we see a long period of restorative waiting while he was a refugee, fleeing from King Saul's anger and jealousy. David easily could have had his followers effect a coup and unseat Saul, but he wanted to do God's will; and so there was a long period of waiting.

Running ahead of God can be disastrous. Remember the Old Testament character of Sarah, wife of Abraham. God had promised that she would have a son, but Sarah got tired of waiting; so she ran ahead of God. She gave her Egyptian maid, Hagar, as a concubine to Abraham to bear a child. Afterward, there was conflict in the home and anguish in Sarah's heart. Worse than that, Hagar's son, Ishmael, grew up to be the leader of the Arabs (see Genesis 21:1-18), and Sarah's son, Isaac, a leader of the Israelites—and the conflict continues. How often I have wondered if things might be different in the Middle East today if Sarah had practiced restorative waiting instead of running ahead of God.

4. Look for Good in the Situation and/or the Person

Jesus had the power to see the good in people and situations. This ability guards the heart and keeps the mind from resentment. This ability to see possibilities in people also affects our attitude toward them. I certainly believe that Jesus understood Simon—his weaknesses as well as his strengths. Yet, Jesus didn't call attention to Simon's impetuousness and his lack of stability. Instead, Jesus gave him a new name, Peter, which is taken from the Greek word *petros*, meaning rock. In that sense, he was naming him what he believed Peter could become. How wonderful it would be if we could do the same thing.

How different our world would be if we could see good in others rather than focusing on what we don't like about them. If we, like Jesus, could see what another person can become rather than what he or she is now, the person could build on strengths rather than strengthen weaknesses.

I've discovered that we usually try to live up to the expectations of people we respect, whether the expectations are high or low. I felt this so strongly in my second job. After serving two years as director of youth ministries in a local church, I was invited to become conference director of youth ministries in the Western North Carolina Conference of my denomination. I was honored and humbled by the invitation but very apprehensive about my inadequacies. That feeling was heightened when I learned that a well-known and competent person on the national scene had been considered for the job. The fact that I was chosen seemed like a miracle to me.

Carl King had high expectations for his staff, but he believed in us, was quick to praise when we did a good job, and encouraged us when we felt we hadn't done so well. In staff meetings, he was extremely clear about what he expected of us and why. More important, whenever he spoke publicly, it was always with praise for what we were accomplishing. It was powerful motivation that stretched us to become what he envisioned.

Even now, years later, I often give thanks for that wonderful man who was so Christlike in developing and motivating others. Are we like that? Or, do we de-motivate others by criticism, low expectations, or lack of praise and encouragement?

As Christians, we must always work toward reconciliation and peace—toward uniting rather than dividing groups.

Digging a Little Deeper

1. Read 1 Samuel 20:33. What precipitated Saul's anger against his son, Jonathan? Do you think it was Jonathan's friendship with David, Saul's jealousy of David because of his popularity with the people, or both? Why? How did Saul handle his anger? What happened?
2. Can anger ever be good? Explain your response. How are Jesus' anger over the moneychangers in the temple (Matthew 21:12) and Abraham Lincoln's anger over slavery different from Saul's anger toward David and Jonathan?
3. When anger hardens into resentment, how does it hurt us more than the person we resent? Give an example from your own life or the life of someone you know, if possible.
4. Why do you think Jesus suggested that we "settle matters" with an adversary quickly (Matthew 5:25)? What happens when we do not follow this advice?
5. Revenge begets revenge and throws us into a cycle of violence. Read Romans 12:18-19—Paul's advice to the Romans about seeking revenge. Do you think he was right? Why or why not?

6. What else can we do to respond appropriately to our anger?
7. Why is restorative waiting often necessary to keep us from running ahead of God? When have you run ahead of God, and what was the result? When have you practiced restorative waiting, and what was the result?
8. Who in your life has stretched and encouraged you rather than pulling you down? What effect has this person had in your life?

Chapter 8

SLAYING THE GIANT OF JEALOUSY

"Saul has killed his thousands, and David his ten thousands."
(1 Samuel 18:7)

In Shakespeare's drama *Othello*, Iago says to Othello, who was seething with jealous thoughts and actions, "O, beware, my lord, of jealousy. It is the green-eyed monster." All of us have seen otherwise rational, intelligent people who become almost monsterlike when caught in the grip of jealousy.

Jealousy is an emotion experienced by one who perceives that another person is giving something that he or she wants (typically attention, love, or affection) to a third party. I believe there is a distinction between jealousy and envy. Jealousy involves keeping what one has, while envy is the wish to get what one does not have. For example, a child is jealous of his parent's attention given to a sibling, but envious of a friend's new bike. This is such a universal emotion that all of us likely have experienced it at one time or another.

Everyone Experiences Jealousy

My husband, Ralph, and I had two sons born twenty months apart—Rick and Ralph, Jr. We thought we had done a good job preparing Rick for the coming of his new brother. Rick talked excitedly about his new brother and helped us get the nursery ready. For the first couple of weeks after Ralph Jr.'s arrival, things went well. Then Rick began awakening a few minutes ahead of his brother's 2:00 AM feeding, screaming that his legs were hurting. We took him to the pediatrician who, after conducting tests, could find nothing wrong with our son's legs. "It's jealousy," he explained, "and it often happens to young children when a sibling is born."

Stunned, I asked, "What can we do?" He replied with a smile, "Two things. First, spend as much time as possible with Rick during the day and early evening. Play with him, hold him, and read to him. This will reassure him of your love. Second, don't take him up when he cries. Check to be sure he is all right—that he doesn't need to be changed or to have a drink of water—but don't take him out of his bed."

"I can't do that," I said. "He screams, and I feel guilty of child neglect." That kind, wise pediatrician replied bluntly, "Do it!"

Though it was the middle of summer in the days before air conditioning, we closed the windows because Rick's screams were so loud we were certain the neighbors would think we were abusing him.

That first night held the longest fifty minutes of my life. Ralph and I sat, unnerved and perspiring, on the side of our bed in an adjacent room. Finally, Rick went back to sleep. The second night he cried for twenty-five minutes, and the third night he didn't even awaken. What an ordeal! I am convinced that it was intentionally spending more time with Rick during the day that allayed his fears about what he must have perceived as an intruder trying to take his place.

This experience confirms for me the belief that feelings are the same no matter what the age. Here was a toddler who was incapable of articulating his fears that the attention and love given exclusively to him were now being given to another. Our wise pediatrician enabled us to understand the problem and deal with it before it became the seedbed of sibling rivalry.

Jealousy is often a perception, not a fact. Sometimes we can see the perception through a funny or strange incident. With our two little boys, it was an amusing incident when Ralph Jr. was six months old that gave us another insight about Rick's expectation of a new baby brother. Late one afternoon Ralph was putting fertilizer on our not very lush lawn. Rick, following his dad around, asked, "Why are you doing that, Daddy?" Showing our son the picture of a beautiful lawn on the bag of the fertilizer, Ralph replied, "This will make the grass grow."

The following morning, I placed the portable playpen out in the backyard so the baby could get a little suntan. Rick was happily playing in a nearby sandbox. Within a short time, I heard the baby screaming, and I rushed to the playpen. Rick, holding a nearly empty bag, had sprinkled the fertilizer all over his brother. "Make him grow, Mommy," he declared with his eyes dancing. Suddenly, I realized that our toddler had expected his new brother to be his size and was disappointed that he was so small. As you can imagine, the baby did grow up, and the two brothers became great friends.

Jealousy can happen at the other end of the age scale, as well. How well I remember a lovely-looking eighty-year-old woman whose soft, beautifully coiffed hair framed an amazingly unlined face enhanced by softly hued makeup. I had been with her in numerous meetings where her mental sharpness and gracious manner had added immeasurably to our considerations. Imagine my surprise to learn of her sudden hostile actions toward her husband and their older son. In counseling, it became evident that she thought her son was paying more attention to her husband than to her. Jealousy is no respecter of age, gender, or race. From early childhood to senior adulthood, we will experience, sometimes momentarily, feelings of jealousy. This was true even in the first biblical family.

Biblical Examples of Jealousy

In Genesis 4:1-9, we find jealousy in the heart of Cain, the older son of Adam and Eve. Scripture tells us that Cain was a tiller of the soil and Abel was a shepherd boy. As was the custom in that first family, they each brought offerings of their first fruit as a sacrifice to God. After they lighted their sacrifices and watched them burn, Cain perceived that God was more pleased with Abel's sacrifice than with his, so he became jealous. Because he didn't deal with his jealousy, it festered and grew stronger. Then, one day when the two brothers were in the field, Cain suddenly turned on Abel and killed him.

When God asked, "Cain, where is your brother, Abel?" Cain replied with those infamous words, "I do not know; am I my brother's keeper?" (Genesis 4:9). Because he couldn't control his jealousy, Cain was banished from the garden and became a wanderer throughout the earth. When we hurt another person because of jealousy, we inevitably cause harm to ourselves. Even when the harm is not obvious to others, the jealous person cannot experience peace of mind.

Another tragic and picturesque example of the effects of jealousy is found in today's scripture. King Saul was so pleased when the teenaged David killed the Philistine giant, Goliath, that he gave David a large purse of money, one of his daughters (Michal) in marriage, and exemption from paying taxes.

After slaying Goliath, David joined the Israelite army in pursuing and conquering the Philistines. Saul's army returned in triumphal procession. As they processed, the townspeople came out en masse, and the women began to chant, "Saul has killed his thousands, and David his ten thousands" (1 Samuel 18:7). Saul heard the chant and was filled with fury and jealousy.

Even after David's marriage to Saul's daughter, the green-eyed monster stayed with the king until his peace of mind was completely destroyed. As a result, David became a refugee from the kingdom and was pursued madly by Saul until the king's death.

To David's credit, he never attempted to kill Saul even though he had ample opportunity. In fact, David forgave the king and united the kingdom. It is not surprising that he is still known as Israel's greatest king.

Another biblical example of jealousy can be seen in the New Testament. Although the scripture does not specifically mention jealousy, I believe that jealousy was part of the reason that the disciples first would not accept Paul. Here were good and faithful disciples who followed and supported Jesus in good times and bad. Suddenly, a man who had fought the Christian movement claimed to have been converted and wanted to be a partner with them. It was Barnabas, the encourager, who got them to accept Paul. Shortly thereafter, Paul's impassioned preaching created a following for him—and a controversy. Was it jealousy that caused them to send him back to Tarsus and to leave him there for ten years?

It was Barnabas, not the disciples, who went to Tarsus and asked Paul to join him at Antioch. I believe that those courageous disciples may have had, at least for a short time, some of the jealous feelings of the elder brother in the parable of the prodigal son (see Luke 15:25-32).

Jealousy Is a "Disease"

Once I heard William Sangster, British minister and author, preach for a week in America. One of his topics was jealousy, which he described as the "saddest sickness of the human mind."

In my senior year in college, I experienced in a very small way an example of jealousy as a disease. I ran for, and was elected to, a major office on campus. My opponent was a girl I had tried to befriend when she transferred to our college in her junior year. For some reason, she seemed to be jealous of my friendship with others. She tried in subtle and devious ways to destroy my friendships. I tried everything from kindness to confrontation to help her know that I wanted to be her friend. Nothing worked!

When I was nominated for president of an organization that would demand lots of time and effort, she immediately announced her own candidacy. Because she had no track record and few friends, she was overwhelmingly defeated. That only intensified her desire to have whatever I had. She was like a dog that wouldn't turn loose the bone. It was a constant irritation to me. Several months before we were to graduate, she was diagnosed with mental illness and had to leave school. It was only then that I understood that Sangster was right—jealousy can become a disease.

After years of study of the "disease," Sangster made some observations that can keep us from reacting negatively when someone is jealous of us:

Observation #1: Jealousy Is the Backwash of Personal Insecurity

Following the assassination of President John F. Kennedy, I was curious about why Lee Harvey Oswald would perform such a dastardly act. Was it politics? I wondered. Did he represent a hate group whose members despised the president's stand on civil rights and labor? Or was Oswald targeting Governor Connally rather than President Kennedy? I read every account I could find about the assassin, and most writers agreed that it was the personal insecurity of Oswald that produced jealousy of the man who had everything he longed for—love of family and friends, wealth, good looks, prestige, and power.

I discovered that Oswald's father had died before Lee Harvey was born. His mother was an unhappy woman who obviously didn't want a child, and she worked outside the home for most of every day. Not having any relational skills, young Oswald had no friends. In fact, a school counselor was reported to have written that the student didn't even know the meaning of the word love.

Though he had a high I.Q., Oswald dropped out of high school and joined the Marines. Even there, he was dishonorably discharged because of fighting and resistance to officers' commands. He went to Russia where he met and married a girl with a similar background.

When they returned to the United States, they lived in Dallas, but were soon separated. On the day before the assassination, he had gone to plead with his wife to take him back. She refused, ridiculing him in front of her friends. He calmly went to the garage and took down a rifle, which he carried to work with him the following day. In pulling the trigger of that rifle, he may have done the only thing he had learned to do well in all of his miserable life.

While this is an unusual and tragic example, it emphasizes the urgent need for children to have love and acceptance, and for them to develop skills for living effectively in our world. The more we believe in ourselves, the easier it is for us to accept others. This is why the Christian faith is so important in developing personal wholeness and freedom from insecurity.

Sangster emphasized that, as Christians, we need to find our security in what Christ has done for us. In the crucifixion, death, and resurrection of Jesus, we know that we are loved, redeemed, and empowered for whatever life demands. Christ has freed us from insecurity and inferiority, and the following observations can help us understand why we are dealing with a green-eyed monster.

When we recognize and believe that Christ gave up his life for us, then we understand fully the height and depth of God's love for us as individuals. This provides not only the twin gifts of salvation and eternal life, but also the incredible power of belief in ourselves and in our potential.

There was a young woman named Kathy whose harsh home life had created feelings of insecurity and fear. It was a Sunday school teacher, Mrs. Parsons, who helped her know what Christ has done for each of us. Parsons helped the child develop relational skills— and even helped Kathy's mother develop parenting skills. Kathy grew in confidence in Sunday school and church. She went from a shy, insecure child to a radiant, confident young woman who exuded energy and joy. This happened because a Sunday school teacher helped her internalize the love of God through Christ.

Observation #2: Jealousy Is Displeasure or Regret Aroused by What We Perceive as the Superiority of Another

Ralph Waldo Emerson is credited with this quotation: "Every man is in some way my superior and in that, I learn of him." Unfortunately, in our insecurity we often resent, become jealous of, or compete with others. If we could only appreciate them and learn from them, our lives could be enormously richer. We need, also, to remember that in some ways we are superior to others. My high school English teacher often said to her students, "Accentuate your strengths and work to change your weaknesses." Following this advice, we can constantly work toward overcoming our insecurities. In addition, we can be a Barnabas to those who need our encouragement.

If we don't do this, we may view anyone we perceive to be superior with resentment and jealousy. Acts of revenge sometimes follow—either because we feel powerless, as in the case of Lee Harvey Oswald, because there is intense competition. The case of one mom is an illustration of the latter. She so wanted her daughter to be the head cheerleader that she had her daughter's competition badly injured in order to assure that result.

Sangster has said that when revenge beckons us, we need to work to become more and more Christlike in our living. Also, Jeremiah 29:11 reminds us of God's plans for our lives: "For surely I know the plans I have for you, says the LORD, plans for your welfare and not for harm, to give you a future with hope."

When we find God's purpose for our lives, we feel what Eric Liddell called "God's pleasure" in the Academy Award-winning movie *Chariots of Fire*. Liddell's sister, Jenny, became concerned that Eric was spending so much time running as he practiced for the Olympics that he would forget his calling. His reply was, "Jenny, I believe God made me for a purpose, but he also made me fast; and when I run, I feel God's pleasure."

As committed Christians, we all feel God's pleasure at times. Sometimes it is in our role as parents interacting with our children; sometimes it is in our business or professional or church life. At this time in my life as a speaker and author, I feel "God's pleasure" when I connect at a deep level with an audience or when I receive a note or e-mail from someone who has been helped by my books.

Sangster has said that we need to work toward our own spiritual maturity and stop comparing ourselves with others. God has a purpose for each of us. We need to discover our purpose rather than try to sabotage that of another.

Observation #3: Jealousy Is More Common in Middle Age than in One's Youth or Senior Years

Though Sangster didn't give reasons for this observation, I don't completely agree with him. Jealousy is seen in children, youth, and young adults, as well as in those who are middle-aged. During my third- to fifth-grade years, a new girl who had moved to our community became my competitor for academic achievement. Since I had enjoyed the top academic position before her arrival, I resented her being in the class. When she won our teacher's accolades, I felt real jealousy. Fortunately our teacher recognized the competition and complimented each of us when averages were announced. She also had the two of us work together on projects. The girl and I became great friends even into our college years.

Later as a youth director, I realized how prevalent jealousy is among teenagers—boys as well as girls. Often at that age, jealousy centers around popularity and dating experiences more than academic achievement. It can be very hurtful to young people and have a negative effect on self-image.

Young adult couples seem to be more into envy than jealousy— envying those who have a larger house, more money, a better job, and more invitations to parties. Even so, jealousy can be felt strongly during young adult years.

Perhaps Sangster felt that it is in midlife that jealousy has a more long-lasting effect. Often middle-aged persons begin to grow bitter because they either lose hope or just give up. We must not let it happen! Instead, as we assess our lives at "halftime," we must evaluate how we have done with the goals we set as young adults. It may surprise us how much we have accomplished by this time in our lives, so we should give thanks to God for opening doors and blessing us. As our children are older now and life's circumstances have changed, it is time to set new goals. But we must be sure that these goals are set in light of the Christian faith and what we deeply desire.

At whatever age, life will be full of challenges, but God's peace will remain with us if we stay focused on God's priorities—faith, family, our calling, friends, and service. Continue to ask, "Lord, what will you have me to do with the rest of my life?" Then remember, "Nothing is impossible with God" (Luke 1:37 NIV).

Observation #4: Jealousy Operates within Groups, Professions, and Classes

Sangster suggests that though there may be envy between members of different professions, most often jealousy operates within the same group or profession. One reason, of course, is that two people may be considered for one position, so there is competition. Also, most professions have associations or some other kind of organization that compares one professional with another, which may stimulate jealousy. It takes a strong, self-confident Christian to keep his or her focus on God's purpose rather than on the competition.

Observation #5: Jealousy Operates against People Who Have Similar Attributes and Opportunities as We Do, but Who Have Surpassed Us Slightly

For example, an actress in a local theatre group is not jealous of Julia Roberts or Meryl Streep. Instead, she is jealous of a local actress who got the part in the play that she wanted. An actress friend told me that she can learn from national stars such as Roberts and Streep, but she resents people who are no more talented than she yet who still move ahead of her. If she could remember Jesus' command to "Love one another" (John 13:34), she could learn from her competitor and perhaps gain a new friend.

Observation #6: Jealousy Operates within Extended Families and Groups of Friends

When children grow up, get married, and later have their own children, jealousy can rear its ugly head. An example of this is fresh in my mind, because a former neighbor had a close-knit family that included three fine children. After all three married, the dynamics of the family changed drastically. One son-in-law is extremely jealous of the other two families—of their accomplishments, their professional success, and their material possessions. The parents feel that this is because of the dysfunctional home in which the young man grew up. Yet, he refuses to go for counseling, and thus his own children live in a far-from-loving home. There are no more family reunions as before. The three households come separately to the parents' home for visits. If the jealous man's marriage survives the stresses, it will be a miracle. His wife is deprived of the closeness she used to feel toward her sister and brother.

"Are they Christian?" you may ask. That unhappy little family does go to church regularly; but for the husband, the faith is a ritualistic religion, not a relationship with Jesus Christ.

Unfortunately, the same kind of thing can happen to a group of friends when jealousy is among them.

Sangster has suggested that we need to love and regularly pray for each member of the family and for our friends. Prayer actually communicates loving and peaceful thoughts to the jealous person, but it also helps the person who prays to perceive the jealous one with more understanding.

I am such a firm believer in prayer—not only because Jesus modeled for us a life of prayer, but also because of my own experiences. For example, on the night before my first cancer surgery, I felt apprehensive and a little jittery. The next morning I awakened at five-thirty with my mind and heart completely at peace. Only later did I learn that twenty members of my Sunday school class had arrived at the hospital chapel at five AM to start praying for me.

They remained during the five-hour surgery. Their prayers became the "wind beneath my wings" during long months of recovery. I felt totally surrounded by prayers from them and many others. Over and over in family crises and on ordinary days, our family has felt the power of prayer. In fact, I recommend that you keep a journal of prayer requests and when and how the prayers are answered. As the old hymn tells us, "It will surprise you what the Lord has done." Even a jealous person can be reached through prayer.

Sangster also has emphasized that we should not do anything to provoke jealousy—such as boasting or showing off new purchases that other family members or friends do not have. Instead, we need to take the spotlight off ourselves and show genuine interest in others.

My husband's brother was a very successful businessman who never flaunted his possessions but shared them with great generosity. Many newlyweds in our extended family used his beautiful condo in Florida for honeymoons. His large cabin cruiser and lovely home in Lexington, Kentucky, were always available for family events. No one was ever jealous of Phil—only grateful for his magnanimity.

Cultivating the Christian attribute of humility allows us to avoid provoking jealousy in others. We need to remember that all we have comes from God—our talents, possessions, and opportunities. Knowing this leaves no room for arrogance. We are blessed to be a blessing!

Observation #7: Jealousy Is So Penetrating and Pervasive a Disease that Only the Divine Physician Is Able to Heal It

Perhaps I have spent so much space talking about the destructive emotion of jealousy because it almost "sank my ship." Before marriage, I was a conference director of youth ministry, a job I enjoyed and felt confident to do. I had family in a nearby town, lots of friends, and money to do with as I pleased. When I married a young pastor, I moved to another state—away from all the things that had held me up. I changed my job for one that required domestic skills I didn't have. In addition, our first child was born just before our first wedding anniversary.

In the midst of my insecurity, jealousy attacked me. I was jealous of the fresh air my husband breathed, of the enormous amount of time he had to spend in church activities, and of the necessary attention he gave to church members. My husband helped me tremendously by his affirmation, by finding places where my talents could be used, and by making our time together full of love, joy, and fun.

Most of all, I knew that I had to move my faith in Christ up a notch. Up to that time, Christ had been my friend and Savior. It was in my extremity that Jesus came in power when I turned my entire life over to him as Lord. One morning in desperation, I prayed, "Lord, if you can do anything with this warped personality of mine, you may have it as long as I live." It was the beginning of a long healing for most of my jealous thoughts. Later I would be able to write: "Anytime that we touch even the hem of his garment in desperate believing faith, we can be made whole." Indeed, it is the divine physician who does the healing at a very deep level.

How Jesus Dealt with Jealousy

Jesus was the victim of jealousy throughout his short ministry. When he came to Jerusalem to attend his last Passover Feast, Caiaphas was the high priest in Jerusalem. Whereas most other high priests had served in that office for one year, Caiaphas had held the position for eighteen years and felt that he had the last word in religious matters. When people began to follow Jesus in great crowds, Caiaphas was overwhelmed with jealousy. He and his friends and relatives in the Sanhedrin plotted to destroy Jesus (see Matthew 26:3-4).

How did Jesus react? First, he stood firm about what he believed was the will of God. For example, he set his face to go to Jerusalem (see Luke 9:51). Even though it would have been safer to stay away from that city, Jesus believed this to be the plan of God, and he never wavered. Second, he forgave those who would destroy him. Most important, he surrendered his life and actions into the hands of God, praying, "Nevertheless not my will, but thine, be done" (Luke 22:42 KJV). The glorious truth is that God took the worst that the world could do to Jesus and turned it into the magnificent truth of the Resurrection. As a result, we are all "more than conquerors through him who loved us" (Romans 8:37).

The way Jesus handled the jealousy of others was to stay close to God in prayer. After meeting the needs of the people, he regularly went to a quiet place for prayer. I'm convinced that the only enduring way we overcome jealousy is to allow Christ to live in us.

Jealousy and the Marriage Relationship

Though jealousy can be experienced in friendships, family relationships, work relationships, and even relationships among those with a shared hobby, perhaps it is felt most painfully if a third person is perceived to be a threat to the marriage relationship. A third person intruding in what Christians believe to be an exclusive relationship is causing many divorces today, which is why I have chosen to address this relationship specifically.

When God made a covenant with the people of Israel, he declared that he was a jealous God and that they were to have no other gods before him (see Exodus 34:14). As Christians, we enter into this covenant when we acknowledge Jesus as Savior and Lord. A covenant between us and God, through Christ, is an exclusive relationship.

Similarly, a marriage is a relationship between God and the couple. In the marriage ceremony, the couple promises to "forsake all others" and to keep the emotional and sexual love between the husband and wife as an exclusive relationship—a relationship that should be guarded with their very lives. Trust is the element that ensures the relationship and holds jealousy at bay.

In a day when sex is often considered a recreational activity to be engaged in with as many partners as you like—a day when affairs seem to be a dime a dozen in television shows, movies, and real life—Christians should take certain precautions to avoid sexual temptation.

1. Don't allow yourself to work late with a person to whom you feel some kind of emotional or physical attraction.
2. Don't allow yourself to have a business luncheon alone with someone whom you may be attracted to, or someone you feel is attracted to you.

3. Avoid off-colored jokes, innuendos, and suggestions that might be considered sexual harassment.
4. Keep your home fires burning brightly. In the midst of busyness with social, community, church, and children's activities, the husband and wife must make time for their inner worlds to "touch." Here are a few suggestions:

- Keep the romance alive.
- Have a date night at least once every two weeks. Don't talk about household matters or plans for the children. Focus on each other and have fun.
- Remember why you fell in love with your spouse.
- Avoid boredom in the bedroom.
- Remember that your marriage is like a triangle with Christ at the top and you and your spouse at the base. The closer you come to Christ individually, the closer you come to each other.
- Keep your family actively involved in church. Friends who share your faith provide a wonderful support system.

Let us remember that there are many ways to betray a spouse in addition to sexual unfaithfulness. Betrayal can be the verbal putting down of a marriage partner, trying to control a spouse's actions, talking about a spouse's intimate life to others, or treating a spouse in a patronizing manner. Christian marriage is a partnership, not a one-man or one-woman show.

Overcoming Jealousy

We have seen that jealousy is a complex emotion that arises when we feel someone is getting something we want from a third person—usually attention, love, or affection. Unless we learn to control the emotion, it will grow and become "one of the saddest diseases of the human mind." Jealousy leads to conflict, anger, resentment, and sometimes even physical injury and death.

If your jealousy stems from childhood issues or is delusional or unmanageable, see a Christian psychiatrist. Delusional jealousy is a psychiatric disorder called the Othello Syndrome. It is named for Shakespeare's Othello, who murdered his wife because of his false belief that she had been unfaithful.

King Saul destroyed himself, not David, through the jealousy he allowed to grow and fester. We, too, can destroy ourselves with jealousy if we refuse to deal with it. We must face it and work to overcome it with God's help. First, we must renew our commitment to Christ and allow him to empower us to work toward personal wholeness. We also need to avoid comparing ourselves with others and, instead, begin to discover, cultivate, and use our unique gifts. This will enable us to serve others and grow in our own confidence. Thus, we will have Christ-centered confidence rather than self-confidence. As Sangster suggested, only Christ, the great physician, can heal the disease of jealousy. We must stay close to the physician!

Digging a Little Deeper

1. Violence is sometimes a result of jealousy. Read Genesis 3:1-9. Why did Cain kill Abel in a jealous rage? Have you ever felt so resentful and jealous of someone that you wanted to harm the person? What did you do?
2. Read 1 Samuel 18:7. What sparked King Saul's jealousy? Was it David's actions in battle or the response of the people? How did Saul handle his jealousy? What happened as a result?
3. William Sangster describes jealousy as the "backwash of personal insecurity." Describe a time when you were jealous of someone because of insecurity. What can we do to avoid this problem?
4. What is the quality in a marriage that will protect the relationship from jealousy or third-party interference? How can a couple cultivate this quality in their marriage?
5. What does the symbolism of a triangle—with Christ at the top and the husband and wife at the base—say to you about marriage? What can a couple do to keep Christ at the top, or center, of their relationship?
6. Name one thing you can do when you feel the green-eyed monster attacking you.

Chapter 9

SLAYING THE GIANT OF LUST

It happened, late one afternoon, that when David rose from his couch and was walking about on the roof of the king's house, that he saw from the roof a woman bathing; the woman was very beautiful.   *(2 Samuel 11:2)*

The giant of lust seems to be as old as biblical times and as current as the morning newspaper or television newscast. Before I began writing this chapter, the news waves were filled with reports of the sexual indiscretion of a well-known and popular pastor of a huge nondenominational church. This revelation was a jolt to the entire Christian community. It represents a betrayal of the marriage covenant, which for Christians includes a covenant with God. As shocking as the news is to Christians who don't even know him, how much greater is the hurt to his wife and five children and members of his congregation who loved and trusted him.

A national news show broadcast did an entire segment on marital infidelity. Though they didn't indicate their sources, the reporters said that in 65 percent of the married couples in America there either had been, was now, or would be an affair. There's no question that the problem of infidelity in marriage, prompted by the giant of our lust, is prevalent in our society.

In a book entitled *The American Sex Revolution* (Porter Sargent Press, 1956), Pitirim Sorokin, professor of sociology at Harvard University, called our culture a "sex-saturated, sensate society," and he predicted some of the results we see today: a rise in homosexuality, infidelity in marriage, children born out of wedlock, couples living together without the benefit of marriage, and sexually transmitted diseases.

Another growing problem identified with lust is pornography, which includes voyeurism, an exaggerated interest in viewing sexual objects to obtain sexual gratification. In the past this may have meant being a peeping tom or reading sexual magazines, but today, with advanced technology, the problem centers around the Internet. The size of this problem is reflected in recent statistics reporting that pornography is more than a $57 billion industry worldwide—with approximately $12 billion generated in the United States. Most alarming to me is the fact that the largest consumer of Internet pornography is in the twelve-to-seventeen age group, while forty million adults regularly visit pornography Web sites.

Michael Leahy, a former pornography addict, says that his addiction cost him his fifteen-year marriage, a career, friendships, and his family life with his two sons. On the brink of suicide, he turned his life over to Christ. He is now sharing his story with thousands of college students throughout the United States in a "Porn Nation Tour" sponsored by Campus Crusade for Christ.

I'm familiar with the devastating effects of pornography addiction because I have watched as a wonderful young family was torn apart by a husband's addiction to Internet pornography. The couple appeared to have a picture perfect marriage. They had been pillars of their church, serving as co-presidents of a large class for couples, and they were active participants in marriage and family programs. Their two attractive children received perfect attendance awards at Sunday school for many years.

Then the husband began to get interested in Internet pornography. When his wife, his parents, and his pastor confronted him, he told them that he had given up pornography. Actually, he simply had moved his place of viewing to his office, which later resulted in the loss of his job. Even addiction counseling seemed to have little effect. Eventually he began to have illicit liaisons with women, some of whom were prostitutes.

The wife stayed in the marriage, prayed for her husband, and believed that the fine man she had married would emerge again. It was when she realized the disastrous result her husband's behavior was having on their children that she regretfully ended the marriage. Today he is living on a small trust fund from his parents and has no contact with his children. It has been a total disintegration of a personality. Gradually he became addicted to pornography and, just as gradually, he became anaesthetized so that he saw nothing wrong with his actions.

Is it possible that we as a nation also have become anesthetized to the problem—to the enormity of the giant of lust? If you have ever been anesthetized, you know that the drugs cause you to lose your sense of feeling—and sometimes your capability of responding. For example, when your dentist puts a shot of Novocain in your gums, it renders you incapable of feeling the pain you would have experienced without the shot. When you are being prepared for surgery, it is amazing how quickly you are under the influence of the drug administered. A surgeon can cut into your body without you feeling any of the pain.

It occurs to me that we may have been morally and spiritually anesthetized to lust, incapable of responding spiritually to this giant as we should. How could this have happened to us? The answer, of course, is gradually. Often we accept, over a period of time, that which we would never accept suddenly.

There is a classic psychological experiment that validates this point. A frog was placed in a pan of cold water, and then the pan was placed on the stove. Very slowly and imperceptibly, the temperature of the water was raised. Eventually, the temperature reached the boiling point. Yet it was done so gradually that the frog made no effort to escape.

Similarly, the changes that occur in our society often happen so gradually that there is no recognition of the danger. This problem affects the fabric of our nation whether or not we are involved individually. As the opening scripture for this chapter indicates, a good person can subtly become a victim of lust.

David Struggled with the Giant of Lust

As we have looked at the life of David, from his early life as a shepherd boy to his ascendancy to the throne of Israel, we have seen one who was a sincere and faithful follower of the one true God. Yet the giant of lust not only tempted this mighty king but also created a black chapter in an otherwise blameless career. Nevertheless, it was David's genuine sorrow for his sin, his quick seeking of forgiveness, and his beautiful spirit in facing the inevitable results of his indiscretion that opened him to receive God's redeeming grace. David's humble, repentant heart can be seen in his psalms of repentance.

Let's take a look at a brief summary of the drama of David and Bathsheba and consider what we can learn from it.

The Prologue: David Is Ripe for Temptation

The temptation of the eye is a part of our physical heritage, and not sin. David's lustful thoughts when he looked at Bathsheba were not sin until he nurtured the thoughts. As one pastor declared, "You can't keep a bird from flying over your head, but you can keep it from making a nest in your hair."

The lustful thought is the threshold to sin. It is to be fought against as contrary to the will of God. David had the choice of embracing or rejecting his lustful thoughts about Uriah's wife.

The inner decision to dwell on the thought is sin. This is what Jesus tells us in the Sermon on the Mount. In Matthew 5:28, Jesus says that the sin of adultery begins the moment when a person decides to embrace the thought. David's sin of adultery began when he decided to send for Bathsheba. Up until that point, he could have changed his thoughts at any time.

Act 1: David Yields to Temptation

Scene 1

It was a late spring afternoon, a time when most kings were off to battle after the heavy rains had ceased. That year David remained in Jerusalem (see 2 Samuel 11:1). We have no idea why he didn't join his army in battle. Maybe he was tired of fighting or was simply bored. Lust often attacks those who allow themselves to be restless or bored.

Scene 2

David walked out on the rooftop of the king's palace and looked down on a house where a beautiful woman, named Bathsheba, was taking a bath (see 2 Samuel 11:2). According to scholars, Uriah's house must have been built in the manner of most Middle Eastern homes at that time, with a central courtyard that was left open to the sky (*Interpreter's Bible*, Vol. 2, Abingdon Press, 1998, p. 1099). It was in such a courtyard that most people bathed. Since the king's palace was the tallest in Jerusalem, the king could easily see the surrounding homes.

Scene 3

Bathsheba obviously did not set out to seduce David. She was simply taking a bath. It was David's lust, provoked by his probable boredom and his visual stimulation that caused him to send for Bathsheba. For her, it was a command performance. You simply didn't say "no" to the king. They slept together, and Bathsheba became pregnant.

Act 2: David Heaps Sin upon Sin

Scene 1

King David, knowing that Bathsheba's husband, Uriah, was serving in the army, directed Joab, the commander, to send the soldier home for a few days. David questioned Uriah about how the battle was going and then sent him home to be with his wife. David's assumption was that everyone would think the baby was Uriah's. David's clever stratagem was to protect Uriah and Bathsheba, as well as himself, but it didn't work.

Scene 2

Uriah slept on the steps of the king's palace and didn't return to his home because of his high-minded belief that he shouldn't be enjoying time with his wife while the battle for the nation was still in progress.

Scene 3

Seeing no other alternative, David signed Uriah's death warrant by having Joab send the soldier to the front lines during a furious battle. As one commentator has noted, "Sin is like quicksand. The more energetic the human effort to extricate oneself, the deeper the involvement" (*Interpreter's Bible,* Vol. 2, Abingdon Press, 1953, p. 1098).

Scene 4

Uriah was killed, and after a short period of mourning, Bathsheba came to the palace as David's wife. Obviously, David took her as his wife to protect himself, as well as Bathsheba and the unborn child.

Act 3: The Consequences of David's Sin

Scene 1

There was in the kingdom a fearless prophet named Nathan. He discerned what David had done, and God sent him to confront the king to say that God is not mocked. Nathan told David a story about a rich man who had many flocks and herds, and a poor man who had only one ewe lamb. When the rich man had a visitor, he didn't kill any of his flock to serve the man; instead, he killed the one lamb that belonged to the poor man. Then Nathan asked what should be done to the rich man who had done such a dastardly act. David's response was immediate: the rich man should die.

Immediately Nathan pointed his bony finger at the king and said, "You are the man." David had inadvertently condemned himself, and his response was, "I have sinned." Nathan then told him that the king would not die, but that the child whom he had with Bathsheba would surely die. James 1:15 is a fitting description of this scenario: "Then, when that desire has conceived, it gives birth to sin, and that sin, when it is fully grown, gives birth to death."

Epilogue

God's mercy brought good out of evil. The second child of David and Bathsheba was Solomon, whose name meant "favored of God." The forgiveness of God utilized the result of David's sin for the advancement of God's sovereign purposes for David's kingdom.

For me, there are two strong lessons from King David's high-profile sin. First, no matter how righteous we have been, we all are susceptible to temptation unless our relationship to God through Christ is kept current daily. Second, God can use what he didn't choose. If we truly repent, then God's forgiveness and grace can make something beautiful of our lives. David's story must have influenced the early Christian leaders in their strong stand on impurity.

The Early Church and the Giant of Lust

From its inception, Christianity espoused the ideal of chastity—an ideal that had served as a guideline for human society since the giving of the Ten Commandments. This ideal helped to identify what is right and wrong. It advocated purity, the virtue of decency, which includes freedom from any unlawful or immoral sexual experience.

Chastity was an especially controversial ideal during the early days of the church, for immorality was like a cataract of evil at that time. Rome had conquered the world, from which unlimited riches flowed. Luxury, more deadly than any foe, had laid her hand upon the empire and had avenged the conquered world. Although militarily Rome had conquered Greece, Greek morals had conquered Rome. Rome's victory ruined Rome's character. The result was a revolution against the restrictions of marriage. It was a time of almost universal prostitution and affairs outside the marriage relationship.

Despite the decadent moral climate, early Christians had an uncompromising demand for purity. In his letter to the Ephesians, Paul says that an immoral or an impure person has no share in the Kingdom of Christ and God (see Ephesians 5:5). In writing to the

Colossians, he says that immorality and impurity and passion and evil desires must be inwardly put to death (see Colossians 3:5). Jesus himself said, "Blessed are the pure in heart, for they will see God" (Matthew 5:8).

The rationale for this concept is that, for the Christian, the body is the temple of the Holy Spirit. In 1 Corinthians 6:19, Paul writes, "Do you not know that your body is a temple of the Holy Spirit within you, which you have from God, and that you are not your own?" Christians were asked to glorify God in their bodies. In Romans 12:1, Paul writes, "I appeal to you therefore, brothers and sisters, by the mercies of God, to present your bodies as a living sacrifice, holy and acceptable to God, which is your spiritual worship."

Marriage for the Christian is a sacred and holy estate. As the writer of Hebrews said, "Let marriage be held in honor by all, and let the marriage bed be kept undefiled; for God will judge fornicators and adulterers" (13:4). The final judgment is not the only judgment plaguing some who are sexually promiscuous. The judgment often comes in the breakup of a marriage, the loss of respect of children, internal tension and guilt, and great pain in the lives of those who love the adulterer.

Yet, despite their stand on sexual purity, the early church leaders continually had to deal with the problem. The reason: the culture was sex saturated, and individually, some believers allowed their carnal natures to supersede their spiritual natures. These are the same reasons that the Christian church today struggles with the problem of immorality. Technology has only intensified the problem. Wherever we find promiscuity, it has occurred because someone has succumbed to the giant of lust.

Promiscuity Leads to Guilt and Internal Chaos

Sanjay Gupta, CNN senior medical correspondent, reported in a segment on health and happiness that the married couples who are healthiest and happiest are those who practice fidelity in marriage (series aired November 13–17, 2006). Promiscuity—engaging in sexual intercourse indiscriminately or with more than one partner, either in or out of the marriage relationship—causes not only disease but also an inordinate amount of tension and guilt. The inference is that as the problem increases, the fallout causes our society to become less and less stable.

In her book *Unfinished Business: Pressure Points in the Lives of Women* (Random House, 1995), Maggie Scharf describes her feelings of unworthiness as a result of promiscuity. Sandy, a divorcee of one year, tells of going to bed with many different partners and feeling worse all the time. Her respect for herself had plummeted. She felt cheap and disposable. There was a sense of shame and self-hatred.

Though she had a good job and was financially independent, her promiscuity caused her to feel "rotten and cheap." She said that she felt like a thing that had been passed from person to person and was not worth much to anyone. Intellectually, she could defend eloquently her right and her freedom to do as she chose. Deep inside her, however, there was another set of values clamoring to be heard. She needed security, real love, and to be in a trusting relationship.

Promiscuity has been compared to amphetamines, which may promote a short-term high but can never cure the feelings of despair, grief, and depression or meet the basic needs of the human personality. Paul expressed it well when he said, "Do not be deceived; God is not mocked, for you reap whatever you sow. If you sow to your own flesh, you will reap corruption from the flesh; but if you sow to the Spirit, you will reap eternal life from the Spirit" (Galatians 6:7-8).

How Can We Slay the Giant of Lust?

How, then, can we slay this ever-growing giant of lust? In his book *The American Sexual Revolution*, Pitirim Sorokin suggested that we, as a nation, need once again to seek transcendental, spiritual values rather than sensate values. To me, this means such things as keeping our churches Christ-centered with an emphasis on Jesus' teachings on the sanctity of the family. It involves strong premarital counseling, which gives practical help in areas that can destroy love—such as mismanaging finances, using sex as a bargaining chip, not standing together in the valuing and training of children, being selfish, and so forth. It also means supporting couples after they say "I do." Newlyweds need to be surrounded by a whole cadre of couples who have great marriage relationships and loving homes. Young couples need older couples as mentors, and they need to see "the joy of the Lord" in these mentors.

Our churches also must sponsor strong programs that enrich marriage at every stage, as well as programs for our youth on dating and purity. A marriage counselor speaking to our church's youth on "The Challenge of Dating" advised, "You need to make a commitment now to save yourself sexually for the person you will marry instead of trying to deal with it on a moonlit night when you are feeling romantic toward your date." Our young people need to hear practical, biblical advice such as this from caring adults.

This is equally true for the large number of adult singles in our society today. If churches develop programs for singles aimed toward wholeness in every area of life—physically, mentally emotionally, socially, and spiritually—there will be happier, healthier singles. As a result, the marriages they enter will be stronger, healthier, and happier.

There also are practical measures we must take as individuals to protect ourselves against the temptation of lust. First, we must affirm the sanctity of sex within the marriage relationship. This is both an inward and outward affirmation supported not only by our words but also by our actions. As Christians, we affirm the sanctity of sex within marriage when we say in the wedding ceremony, "Forsaking all others, keep thee only unto her/him so long as you both shall live." This helps plant the idea firmly in our minds and hearts. My husband, Ralph, and I—along with many other Christian couples of all ages—reaffirm our marriage vows at each anniversary. This helps reinforce within us the sanctity of marriage in God's sight.

Second, we must decide not to view sexually perverse or inappropriate material on Web sites or in movies, television shows, or magazines. Viewing this kind of material plants pictures of immoral sex acts in our minds. This, I believe, is one of the reasons Paul cautioned the Christians in Rome, "Do not be conformed to this world, but be transformed by the renewing of your minds" (Romans 12:2). He also said to the Christians at Philippi, "Finally, beloved, whatever is true, whatever is honorable, whatever is just, whatever is pure, whatever is pleasing, whatever is commendable, if there is any excellence and if there is anything worthy of praise, think about these things" (Philippians 4:8).

Third, we must decide not to allow ourselves to be in a compromising situation. In business today, men and women often need to work late or travel out of town together. Unless we have decided how to handle a tempting situation long before the opportunity presents itself, it can quickly evolve into a romantic or sexual affair to threaten or even destroy a marriage. The reason for this, of course, is that trust is eroded.

We also must decide not to entertain lustful thoughts in our imaginations. Even imagining ourselves to be in an illicit relationship can destroy our ability to make logical decisions. When imagination battles against logic, imagination always wins. This, I believe, is what Jesus meant when he said, "But I say to you that whoever looks at a woman to lust for her has already committed adultery with her in his heart" (Matthew 5:28 NKJV).

Finally, we must take a strong stand against pornography, including fighting against adult businesses in our communities and indecency on the Internet and in movies, television shows, and magazines. Last year in our city, some adult businesses began to cluster in an area where there were schools and lots of young people. Several incidents and arrests occurred before parents and grandparents organized with a petition and their actual presence at the city council. Eventually the businesses were closed. We can make a difference!

The fight goes on, and at this point, the giant of lust seems to be slaying us. Let us, like David in facing Goliath, go forth in faith and courage to win this battle for all those who will come after us.

Digging a Little Deeper

1. What signs indicate that sex outside the marriage relationship is becoming the norm for our culture? How and why do you think this has happened?
2. Why do you think that King David, who had been a model follower of God, had an impromptu affair with Bathsheba? How might he have resisted this temptation?
3. Why do you think David planned to have Uriah killed? How did God bring good out of this evil?
4. Why was the early Christian's demand for sexual purity so controversial in the Roman world?
5. In her book *Unfinished Business*, Sandy Geller reveals her deep needs. What were they (see p. 111)? Why were they not being met by her promiscuous behavior?
6. How have we as a nation, and even as Christians, been anesthetized to lust and some of its attendant evils? What has caused us to become desensitized?
7. Pitirim Sorokin says that as a nation we need to return to the transcendental, spiritual values proclaimed by Christ in the Sermon on the Mount (Matthew 5–7). In your own words, how would you explain what this means?
8. What are some practical things we as individuals and as a church can do to slay the giant of lust? Name one thing you are or could be working on now.
9. What specific things can your church do to make a difference in this gigantic problem?

Chapter 10

SLAYING THE GIANT OF LONELINESS

Why are you cast down, O my soul, and why are you dis-quieted within me? Hope in God; for I shall again praise him, my help and my God.

(Psalm 42:5-6a)

Loneliness swept all over him. It was more penetrating than the cold, and more enveloping than the darkness." These words from "The Littlest Orphan and the Christ Baby" by Margaret E. Sangster describe the terrible emptiness of a five-year-old child in an English orphanage (originally published in *The Littlest Orphan and Other Christmas Stories*, 1935).

As I remember it, the story tells of a little boy who was brought to the orphanage when he was only a few days old, so he had no memory of living in a home. Some children came to the orphanage when they were seven or eight or even older. When they told stories about eating freshly baked sugar cookies and having bedtime stories read to them, the "littlest orphan" listened in wide-eyed amazement. Some boys were brothers when they arrived at the orphanage, and they shared books and desks and even a bed.

When the dormitory was cold and the matron turned out the lights, that's when the enveloping feeling of loneliness seemed to invade the boy's body as well as his mind. It was then that his eyes searched for the painting of the Christ baby that hung over the mantle. The baby seemed so kind and warm and loving. He had all the qualities for which the little boy so deeply longed. He often thought that if he could bring the painting into the bed with him, he wouldn't feel so cold and lonely.

One night when his hands and feet were freezing and loneliness swept all over him, the littlest orphan crept out of bed and felt his way across the room to the fireplace. But he couldn't even reach the mantle. Slowly and with the utmost quiet, he moved a chair over to the mantle. It was only a small chair, but he was out of breath when he finished. Even so, he was determined to reach the Christ baby, and he pulled and tugged until he finally stood on the narrow mantle and could touch the painting.

The picture was hard and cold, not soft and warm as he had imagined. Still, it was the Christ baby, and so he carefully unwound the wire until he held the painting in his arms. Only then did he think of how he was going to get down. It had been hard enough to get up, but now he had the Christ baby to carry.

At that moment there was a dreaded sound in the hall—a rubber-heeled step. It was the matron making her final rounds of the evening. She pulled open the door, and her flashlight quickly checked all the beds—each but one with a sleeping occupant. He gasped when she found his empty bed. Then, as if pulled by a magnet, her eyes looked directly at the mantle where he stood shivering from fear as much as from the cold.

There was no love in the matron's voice as she said loudly enough to awaken the other children, "Step down at once!" Answering the challenge in her voice, the little boy stepped into the room below and rolled with the Christ baby's splintering picture into the darkness.

The following day, the littlest orphan spent the day in bed with a bruised body and a broken heart. Late in the afternoon, children marched into the dormitory to change their clothes for the Christmas party to be given by the board of trustees. All the trustees would be there, even Mrs. Moore, the lady who had given the picture of the Christ baby. The children had been warned not to speak to the littlest orphan, and they obeyed; but excited, small-boy conversation drifted over to him: "There is a Christmas tree with lights and Santa Claus with presents for everybody." But the littlest orphan didn't even smile. He knew that dire punishment awaited him and there would be no Christ baby to go to for comfort.

Soon after the children left, he heard the sound of the rubber heels in the hall. He slid down in the bed and pulled the covers up so that only his small face was visible. Suddenly, he heard the matron saying in a voice very different from the one she used with the children, "Mrs. Moore, this is John, the boy who deliberately broke the picture of the Christ Child. Now what do you think we should do to him?"

He closed his eyes. If the lady planned to hit him, it would be better to have his eyes closed. Then, in a voice that sounded like velvet, Mrs. Moore said, "Why, he's hurt and frightened, too. Come here, child, I won't hurt you." John opened his eyes to the kind of face that little children dream of—soft skin, a happy smile, and eyes that were kind. He didn't feel frightened at all. Immediately, he got out of bed and stood before her.

Gently she lifted him into her lap. "John," she said in that velvety voice, "you didn't mean to break the picture, did you ?" All day he had lived not only in physical pain but also in the pain of knowing that terrible punishment awaited him. He buried his head in her shoulder and began to sob. (It was the first time he had ever known that ladies have a place in their necks that just fits tiny heads.) "No, ma'am, I didn't mean to break it. I love the Christ baby. It was only because I was so cold and lonely. I just didn't want to be cold and lonely anymore."

Her arms tightened around the frail little boy as she said half aloud and half to herself, "Not to be lonely anymore; to have the nursery open again; to have the Christ child smiling down on a sleeping little boy." She pulled John up so that she could look into his face as she asked, "John, how would you like to go home with me and be my little boy?"

With his eyes dancing and a smile enveloping his bruised face, the five-year-old replied, "Oh, yes, ma'am, I would really like that." Then he nestled back in the arms that held him, and it was Christmas Eve.

This poignant story has always reminded me that loneliness—

that powerful feeling of emptiness and isolation—can happen to anyone, from very young children to teens to adults of all ages.

What Is Loneliness?

In the online encyclopedia Wikipedia, loneliness is described as a feeling of isolation. It is a feeling of being cut off, disconnected, or alienated from other people so that it is difficult to have any form of meaningful human contact. Loneliness should never be equated with being alone. Everyone has times when we are alone for situational reasons or because we have chosen to be alone. Being alone can be experienced as positive, pleasurable, and emotionally refreshing if it is under the individual's control. Jesus regularly pulled away from the crowd for solitude and prayer. Most growing Christians take time daily for quietness and prayer in order to grow spiritually. Loneliness, however, is unwanted solitude.

Supreme Court Justice Oliver Wendell Holmes reportedly said that happiness is having "four feet on a fireplace fender." In other words, togetherness overcomes loneliness and brings happiness. We are made for connectedness and community. One of the saddest affirmations of this appeared in the classified advertisement section of the *Los Angeles Times* several years ago. It was entitled "Rent-a-friend." For a certain amount of money per hour, someone could rent another person just to talk to, or to attend a movie, or have dinner together.

Rupert Brooke, an English poet, told of sailing from Liverpool one day when he felt lonely because everyone else seemed to have someone to whom they were waving goodbye. Rupert hurried down the gangplank, found a dirty little boy and asked, "William, will you wave farewell to me if I pay you a sixpence?" The boy agreed. Soon the whistles were blowing, and the great ship began moving from its berth. William, like the others standing behind the rail on the landing stage, waved and waved. The last object Rupert saw was a dot still faithfully waving a white handkerchief. Even though he had to rent a friend, Rupert momentarily felt connected to another human being.

When we understand the source of our loneliness, it becomes much easier to find a solution to the problem.

The Problem of Loneliness

There are many life situations that precipitate loneliness. Being around other people is only one solution to loneliness. We can feel lonely in a room filled with people when we don't feel accepted, in a chaotic work situation, or in an unhappy marriage or friendship. Here are just a few other examples:

- Children who are abandoned or who feel abandoned, such as those left at an orphanage.
- Children who are neglected or abused or cruelly teased.
- Teens who don't feel accepted by their peers, or who have been exploited or sexually abused in family situations.
- Young people who don't get accepted into their college of choice.
- People who have low self-esteem.
- Couples who live in anger and resentment or a lack of loving communication, or whose marriages end in divorce.
- Individuals who experience the death or extended absence of a spouse, such as occurs with military service.
- People who feel alone in a big city where they know no one.

The very culture in which we live can exacerbate the feeling of loneliness. Some say that loneliness has become a major problem of modern times. At the beginning of the twentieth century, families were typically larger, and very few people lived alone. Today, however, the trend is reversed. In 1995, twenty-four million Americans lived in single-person households. In 1998, over one quarter of the U.S. population lived alone. It is estimated that by 2010, these numbers will have increased to thirty-one million.

This is a place where the church can make a major difference through warm, inclusive worship and programs for all age groups, including a strong ministry to singles. Having worked with singles in a large church for several years, I have seen the value of such a ministry to those who are widowed or divorced and those who have never married. There is a difference, of course, in situational loneliness and chronic loneliness.

Chronic loneliness, as opposed to what each of us feels from time to time, can be life threatening. It is a major risk factor in artery erosion, high blood pressure, stress-related conditions such as obesity and stroke, and depression. Loneliness also can play a part in alcoholism and in hostile and delinquent behaviors of children and adults.

A survey conducted by John Cacioppo, a psychologist at the University of Chicago, reports that doctors say they see much better results from medical care given to patients who have a strong network of family and friends than to patients who are alone. In our fast-paced, technological, and often fragmented world, loneliness is a big problem. What does the Bible say to help us with this problem?

What Does the Bible Say about Loneliness?

Most encyclopedias credit William Shakespeare as having coined the word *lonely* in his play "The Tragedy of Coriolanus" (Act 4, Scene 1). Though the word is not used in scripture, the feelings of loneliness are expressed in many of the psalms. Psalm 42, for example, is directed to those who are lonely or depressed. The psalmist begins by speaking of a longing to feel connected to God. In verses 5 and 11, the psalmist describes the feeling of loneliness and then gives us the cure:

> Why are you cast down, O my soul,
>   and why are you disquieted within me?
> Hope in God; for I shall again praise him,
>   my help and my God.

In the *Confessions of Augustine*, Augustine affirmed the conclusions of Psalm 42 when he wrote, "God has made us for himself and our hearts are restless until they rest in Him" (*World Book*, vol. I, p. 888, 2006). Turning to God, of course, is the first basic step in slaying the giant of loneliness.

In the midst of happy circumstances, we can have a feeling of emptiness and alienation unless we, like the prodigal son (Luke 15:11-24), come to ourselves and return to God through his Son, Jesus Christ.

This happened in my own life. At age fourteen, I committed my life to Christ; and after college I chose to be a director of Christian education in a local church. After three years, I became conference director of youth ministries and then married a young minister. In retrospect, I realize that for years I had been working for Christ but not really living with him in my life. I was still calling all the shots.

In the midst of a happy marriage, and the joy of giving birth to a beautiful, healthy baby boy (except that he had colic for six months), I had a terrible feeling of emptiness and isolation. Some of it, I'm sure, was postpartum depression; but more important, I needed to make Christ the Lord of my life and open every room of my life to his healing presence.

One morning after my husband had left for the office, I knelt beside our unmade bed and prayed the most sincere prayer of my life: "Lord, if you can do anything with this warped personality of mine, you can have it for as long as I live." A feeling of peace and acceptance began to come into every cell of my body. I decided not to tell anyone about my new commitment, but to let it be reflected in my life. Two days later my husband said, "Something has happened to you. You're singing for the first time in months." I had come home to my Source. I wrote in my journal: "When anyone touches even the hem of Christ's garment in desperate believing faith, he or she will be made whole." Though I sometimes have slipped out of fellowship with Christ, I have missed the peace so much that I've quickly returned. Saint Augustine was right, "Our hearts *are* restless unless they rest in him!"

Let's look at other practical steps we can take when facing this giant.

Practical Steps for Slaying the Giant of Loneliness

1. Learn to Love and Respect Yourself

Remember who you are. You are a person of worth who is created in the image of God, redeemed by Christ, and empowered by the Holy Spirit. We all need to work on growing a stronger self-image according to Christian principles. As Edgar A. Guest emphasizes in his poem "Myself,"

> I have to live with myself and so
> I want to be fit for myself to know.

Confident Christians know who they are and have been freed by their faith. It was German philosopher Nietzsche who said, "He who has a 'why' to live for can bear almost any 'how.'" On the Mount of Transfiguration, Jesus fully discovered the "why" of his living and was equipped for all the "how's"—even death on the cross. So it is that Christ frees us from meaninglessness. He gives us a purpose, a sense of mission, a feeling of self worth, a basis for a relationship, and a reason for being. He allows us to see the "whole" of life so that we can live with the mundane without disillusionment.

2. Learn to Love and to Get Along with Others

Learn to put yourself in another's place. See life through his eyes; listen to understand her perspective; accept, encourage, and appreciate the person. Through many years of study, observation, and sometimes painful seeking, I have concluded that you cannot really love another person until you are confident of who you are and have learned to exercise your unique gifts. When you are not threatened or intimidated by another person, you can reach out in acceptance and care enough for that person to be totally present and see life through his or her eyes.

Jesus affirmed people by seeing them as what they were created to be. For example, he called Peter "Rock" long before Peter was a "rock." If we are seeking to be Christlike, we must find ways to follow him in this important task. Some of the things we can do include offering encouragement, giving honest compliments, and helping others get plugged into organizations that can use their gifts.

I know a pastor who does this par excellence. He writes a note of appreciation for the smallest gift given to him or his family, as well as a note of congratulation on a friend's achievement. And he has an amazing ability to match a person's gifts to a position that needs to be filled. The result is not only a strong, growing church, but also a pastor who is greatly loved and respected.

3. Stay Engaged with Life

Get involved! Don't sit back and expect people to come to you. Be a participant in meaningful projects in your church and community. This will help others and bless you in many ways, including making friends and staying connected to others.

A woman in our community is a self-appointed greeter to newcomers in our condominium complex. She takes a plate of fresh-baked cookies and tells the new residents about social and service opportunities. If they are bridge players, she telephones the chair of the bridge groups. She also telephones someone in their church or synagogue of choice. Soon they have as many opportunities to be as involved as they would like. She is never pushy, but always outgoing and caring. Her life is enriched by new friendships, and newcomers don't feel lonely or alienated.

4. Stay Connected to Others

Have you ever wished you could talk with a real person and not a computer voice when you call a doctor's office, the drugstore, or even place an order by telephone? As convenient as e-mail, voice mail, and fax messages are, we feel detached and even lonely unless we have person-to-person contact.

One of the reasons for the popularity of the long-running television show *Cheers* is that it was a place "where everybody knows your name." We are made for community. Jesus commanded us to love one another (John 15:12). Through such groups as Sunday school classes, circles, and prayer groups, caring churches provide food when there is illness or death, and support when there is tragedy or loss of a job. I love the story of the little boy who was afraid of the dark and wanted someone in the family to stay with him until he went to sleep. His mother said, "You don't need to be afraid, God is with you." He replied, "I know, but I want someone with skin on." We all need people "with skin on" to allow us to feel God's love.

All of us—and especially senior adults—need to stay engaged with life in order to maintain mental sharpness and vitality.

5. Be an Active Part of the Body of Christ

The church not only connects us to God through Christ but also teaches us how to care for one another so that the church can become what Paul called "the body of Christ" (1 Corinthians 12:27). Each of us can do our part to help our churches be the true "body of Christ," a place where all participants are welcomed, accepted, and connected as much as they wish to be.

I heard a minister from Oklahoma describe a letter he received from a member of his large congregation. The letter writer said that she hoped members would never stop holding hands when they prayed the Lord's Prayer. Because she was retired and lived alone, that was the only time during the week when she felt the touch of another human being.

Let's help everyone who comes to our churches experience Christian relatedness through acceptance.

6. If Your Loneliness Is Caused by Depression, Seek Medical Help

All of us will feel blue on some days; but when depression becomes chronic, we need to see a physician. The depression may be coming from a physical problem that requires medication. Or, if the depression stems from issues that need to be faced, we may need the help of a counselor in order to make wise decisions.

7. Get a Pet

The Centers for Disease Control recommend pet ownership for the lonely. They suggest that in addition to the companionship that the pet will provide, you will socialize with other pet owners, and consequently you will experience lowered blood pressure and decreased levels of cholesterol and triglycerides. In other words, you will be healthier and less lonely.

Two age groups, seniors and children, seem to be especially helped by owning a pet or having regular contact with one. I have a friend in her late sixties who has gone through some traumatic experiences and physical illnesses. Her dog has been a lifesaver! The unconditional love of that pet has allowed her to maintain her sanity and avoid intense loneliness. It's like having another human being in the apartment.

All of us have probably heard about the amazing results seen when pets have been taken to nursing homes to visit depressed or withdrawn senior adults. Today, however, I heard from a teacher about a new project to help second-grade students read better. Dogs are trained to go into a classroom and lie placidly in front of a young student while he or she reads aloud. All of the students read better when the dog was at their feet, but slow readers were especially improved. The theory is that because the children had no fear of correction, they were able to relax and improve their reading skills.

Indeed, every age group can benefit from the presence of pets.

8. Be Aware of the Holy Spirit's Presence

Remember these words of Jesus: "If you love me, you will keep my commandments. And I will ask the Father, and he will give you another Advocate, to be with you forever. This is the Spirit of truth, whom the world cannot receive, because it neither sees him nor knows him. You know him, because he abides with you, and he will be in you. I will not leave you orphaned" (John 14:15-18a).

As I write this, we are in the midst of the Advent Season, which includes the four weeks before Christmas Day in which we prepare for a worthy celebration of Christ's birth. The message of Advent is "Immanuel: God is with us." This is the message not only of Advent but also of every circumstance of our lives.

A similar message in the song "You'll Never Walk Alone" from the musical *Carousel* is a fitting conclusion. Rodgers and Hammerstein speak of the storms we all encounter in life; then they conclude with these words:

> Walk on, walk on, with hope in your heart,
> And you'll never walk alone.

Digging a Little Deeper

1. What moved you most about the story of "The Littlest Orphan and the Christ Baby"? Why?
2. Did you ever feel lonely as a child? Explain.
3. When did you feel loneliness during your teen years? Explain.
4. Reread the scripture passage for this chapter, Psalm 42:11. As an adult, when have you felt "cast down and disquieted within"? What has helped you to get over this feeling?
5. In your life right now, which of the following do you most need to learn: to love and respect yourself; to love others; or to love and experience God anew? Why?
6. How can you help your church to be a place where visitors and members feel accepted and connected?
7. Read John 4:18. What did Jesus promise? How have you experienced the truth of this promise?